ESTATES IN LAND
AND FUTURE INTERESTS

Problems and Answers

ESTATES IN LAND AND FUTURE INTERESTS

Problems and Answers

Second Edition

JOHN MAKDISI

Professor of Law
University of Tulsa

LITTLE, BROWN AND COMPANY
Boston   New York   Toronto   London

Library of Congress Catalog Card No. 94-79721

ISBN 0-316-54357-8

EB-M

Published simultaneously in Canada
by Little, Brown & Company (Canada) Limited

Printed in the United States of America

To George Lee Haskins, teacher, friend, and scholar, who made Decedents' Estates come alive

Summary of Contents

Contents

Preface

The rules governing estates and future interests stand as relics of the past attempting to serve the needs of the present. Based on the vagaries of historical circumstance, these rules have developed piecemeal into a complicated structure. The arguments of antiquity no longer justify the intricate convolutions that hallmark this area of the law, but time is slow to remove them. Legislation has been enacted in many jurisdictions to simplify and improve the structure, but the common law rules that were a millennium in the making exert considerable control over this area. As a result, these rules continue to haunt the hallowed halls of our law schools, becoming the bane of every law student's existence.

A traditional method of teaching estates and future interests, in a property course or a course on wills, trusts, and estates, traces their historical development from feudal to modern times. This book approaches the matter differently. It focuses on an in-depth study of the rules as they exist here and now. Within the constricted confines of the fundamental courses in this area of the law school curriculum there is no time to do both methods well. An historical approach to estates and future interests is important for a thorough understanding, but it is best left for courses that devote more time to the area. Premised on the idea that it is preferable to understand the "what" well than to understand a whittled "what" and a hurried historical "how," this book has adopted the present-day approach to ensure a firm foundation in the rules.

This book is written specifically as a supplement to be used in conjunction with any property casebook or wills, trusts, and estates casebook. It provides a skeletal systematized account of the common law in its present form interspersed with several problems to flesh out the structure and provide students with a chance to solidify their learning through practice. The second edition to this book removes class gifts from the first chapter and develops it in a second chapter. The first problem set in the first edition has been divided and expanded into the first three problem sets in the second edition. A new chapter and problem set has been added to cover powers of appointment. Altogether 125 new problems and answers have been added to the 300 problems that were in the first edition.

Thus, Chapters 1 through 6 are a brief survey of the rules. Problem sets with fully explained answers are provided at the ends of each of the chapters. For those students who wish a fuller explanation of this area of the law, reference may be made to such texts as Bergin & Haskell's Preface to Estates in Land and Future Interests and Moynihan's Introduction to the Law of Real Property.

Experience over several years has indicated that the rules presented in this book are a mouthful for students to swallow. An effort has been made to organize them in a form that is clear yet concise. In the process some legal concepts and doctrines that are not needed for understanding the fundamental rules of estates and future interests are deliberately omitted. Coverage in this book, for example, does not include an explanation of personal property rules (such as per capita class gifts), marital estates, concurrent estates, lapse, trusts, adoption, the Rule in Clobberie's Case, most of the statutory modifications of common law rules (such as the wait-and-see test for perpetuities), or some of the more sophisticated or collateral rules for construction of ambiguous conveyances (such as implied conditions of survivorship) or perpetuities (such as infectious invalidity and the validity of charitable gifts). It is my firm belief that the surest path to mastery of estates and future interests is to concentrate on the core of the subject presented in this book without too many digressions into ancillary areas until the core is digested.

I wish to thank my former secretary, Rosa DelVecchio, for the many tireless hours she spent typing the manuscript to the first edition. I also wish to thank my Property students over the past 13 years, whose insight and enthusiasm instigated and encouraged my work on this book.

John Makdisi

December 1994

ESTATES IN LAND
AND FUTURE INTERESTS

Problems and Answers

1

Classification of Interests and Estates

The words *estate* and *interest* both describe what a person owns in land. Each describes a different aspect of that ownership. *Estate* describes the nature and extent of an ownership in land. *Interest* describes the relationship of that ownership with other ownerships in the land and the type of person who holds the ownership. In particular, *estate* refers to how an ownership ends, and *interest* refers to how an ownership begins.

A *purchaser* or *grantee* is one who takes an interest by way of inter vivos conveyance or by way of a devise from the *grantor*, but not by way of descent under the laws of intestate succession. (For the sake of convenience, this book often refers to a conveyance without mention of a devise, although the latter transfers an estate just as much as the former.) An *heir* takes an interest from the *intestate* by way of descent.

In most of the conveyances discussed in this book, it is assumed that the grantor owns the whole estate (present interest in fee simple absolute) in the property conveyed. When the grantor owns less than the whole estate (such as a present interest in a life estate or a future interest in a fee simple absolute), the grantor's interest and estate will be specified in the discussion of the conveyance.

A. CATEGORIES OF ESTATES

There are two types of estates, *freehold* and *nonfreehold*. The *freehold estates* (with the words used to create them) are:

(1) *fee simple,* which has the potential of infinite duration and is created by the words "and his heirs" or "and her heirs" or even without any special words (note that words such as "and her

heirs on her father's side" are ineffective to restrict descent and they create only a fee simple absolute):

> "to *A* and her heirs" or "to *A*";

(2) *fee tail,* which has the potential of lasting until the (or a) line of descendants of the purchaser runs out and is created by the words "and heirs of his body" or "and his issue" (note that limitations may be imposed on the line of descendants to restrict it to male or female heirs (estate in tail male or in tail female) or to restrict it to the heirs (or the male or female heirs) of one's body by a particular spouse (fee tail special as opposed to fee tail general)):

> "to *A* and the heirs of her body" or "to *A* and her issue";

(3) *life estate,* which has the potential of lasting until the death of the purchaser or another person (an estate measured by the life or lives of another person or persons is called a *life estate pur autre vie*) and is created by the words "for life":

> "to *A* for life."

The fee tail estate requires special attention to the fact that, although the grantee owns the whole, the grantee cannot dispose of the estate beyond her lifetime because the issue are entitled to inherit the estate until the line of issue runs out. "Issue" is used in this book synonymously with "heirs of the body" to refer to the whole line of one's descendants. The fee tail estate is hardly recognized in the United States today. Statutory provisions often modify or convert this estate into another estate or combination of estates.

The statutes converting a fee tail estate may be divided into four types: (1) The most frequent statutory modification converts it to a fee simple held by the first grantee or devisee. About half the states with statutes of this type also provide that any remainder to follow the fee tail shall be construed as an executory interest in fee simple to become possessory if the first taker dies without lineal descendants. (2) The next most frequent statutory modification converts it to a life estate in the first grantee with a remainder in fee simple absolute to that person's lineal descendants. (3) Another approach gives the first taker a fee tail, but the surviving descendants inherit a fee simple absolute. (4) The least frequent approach recognizes the fee tail estate but permits a tenant in tail (the owner of the fee tail estate) to destroy it by conveying it by deed (albeit not by devise) as an estate in fee simple absolute.

The common law fee tail estate must be understood in order to apply the statutes modifying it. Therefore, this book defines the fee tail estate as it exists at common law. The fee simple conditional, which is hardly recognized in the United States today, is not discussed.

In a conveyance a purchaser/grantee is designated by *words of purchase* and his estate is designated by *words of limitation.* For example, when *O* conveys "to *A* and his heirs," *O* conveys a fee simple absolute to *A.* The words of purchase are "to *A*" and the words of limitation are "and his heirs." When *O* conveys "to *A* and the heirs of his body," *O* conveys a fee tail to *A*. It is important to distinguish between "heirs," "heirs of the body" (equivalent to "issue"), and "children."

Freehold estates are distinguishable from nonfreehold estates in the nature of the holder's right. The holder of a present freehold estate has *ownership* (or, in older terminology, *seisin*). The holder of a present non-freehold estate has a *right to possession*. This right to possession may be called an ownership of a nonfreehold estate, but it is always subject to a greater concurrent ownership in the one holding the freehold estate. This concept of a freehold and a nonfreehold held by different people at the same time in the same property is known more commonly as the land-lord-tenant relationship, wherein the landlord is said to have ownership and the tenant to have possession.

The *nonfreehold estates* are the *term of years, periodic tenancy* and *tenancy at will*. In this book we will be concerned only with the term of years, which has the potential of lasting for a fixed period of time and is created by any words indicating such. For example, when *O* conveys "to *A* and her heirs subject to a term of ten years in *B*," *O* conveys a fee simple absolute to *A* and a term of years to *B*.

B.   SUBCATEGORIES OF ESTATES

Each of the freehold estates may be further subdivided into four categories. Three of these categories contain a condition that, if it occurs, cuts short or gives the grantor the power to cut short the estate. This condition is called a *condition subsequent* (to be distinguished from a condition precedent, which will be explained later in connection with the vesting of future interests). The four categories of each freehold estate are:

(1) ***absolute*** (note that this term is not actually used for a life estate or fee tail), which characterizes an estate without a condition subsequent (note that the only way a fee simple absolute ends is when it has no more takers, and then it escheats to the state):

Fee simple absolute:	"to *A* and her heirs" or "to *A*"
Life estate:	"to *A* for life"
Fee tail:	"to *A* and the heirs of her body";

(2) ***determinable***, which characterizes an estate with a condition subsequent, which, if it occurs, cuts short the estate in favor of the grantor:

Fee simple determinable:	"to *A* as long as *A* does not divorce"
Life estate determinable:	"to *A* for life as long as *A* does not divorce"
Fee tail determinable:	"to *A* and the heirs of her body as long as *A* does not divorce";

(3) ***subject to condition subsequent***, which characterizes an estate with a condition subsequent, which, if it occurs, gives the grantor the power to retake the estate, that is, the condition sub-

sequent in this case does not cut short the estate until the grantor retakes the estate either by making an entry or bringing an action to recover the land:

Fee simple subject to condition subsequent:	"to A, but if A divorces, O may reenter"
Life estate subject to condition subsequent:	"to A for life, but if A divorces, O may reenter"
Fee tail subject to condition subsequent:	"to A and the heirs of her body, but if A divorces, O may reenter";

(4) *subject to executory limitation,* which characterizes an estate with a condition subsequent, which, if it occurs, cuts short the estate in favor of a grantee:

Fee simple subject to executory limitation:	"to A, but if A divorces, then to B" or "to A as long as A does not divorce, otherwise to B"
Life estate subject to executory limitation:	"to A for life, but if A divorces, then to B" or "to A for life as long as A does not divorce, otherwise to B"
Fee tail subject to executory limitation:	"to A and the heirs of her body, but if A divorces, then to B" or "to A and the heirs of her body as long as A does not divorce, otherwise to B."

An estate subject to condition subsequent is distinguished from an estate determinable by the intent of the parties, which in some conveyances may be expressed only in the language of the condition subsequent. Words of *condition* such as "provided that," "on condition that," "if," "but if," and "provided, however," connote an estate subject to condition subsequent. Words of *duration* such as "during," "until," "so long as," "as long as," and "while," connote an estate determinable. Since in an estate subject to condition subsequent the grantor has a power of termination but does not automatically receive a present interest upon the happening of the condition subsequent, words indicating this power, such as "the grantor shall have the right to reenter," also help indicate (and sometimes are required to indicate) the estate. Since the intention of the parties controls, an ambiguity may be clarified by looking to the circumstances of the transaction.

It should be noted that a term of years may be cut short by a condition subsequent in favor of the landlord. This nonfreehold estate is called a *determinable term of years,* but it should not be confused with a freehold estate that is determinable. A nonfreehold estate is concurrent with a freehold estate, contrary to freehold estates that follow each other:

"to A for ten years as long as A does not divorce" (O, the grantor, retains a present interest in fee simple absolute while A holds a determinable term of years.),

"to A and her heirs as long as A does not divorce" (O, the grantor, retains a future interest in fee simple absolute following A's fee simple determinable.).

C. CATEGORIES OF FUTURE INTERESTS

An *interest* may be *present* or *future*. It may exist in either the *grantor* or the *grantee*. A *present interest* is a property right to enjoy ownership at the moment a conveyance takes effect. This interest is vested in possession. A *future interest* is a property right, at the moment of conveyance, to enjoy ownership at some future time. Ownership exists whether one has a present or a future interest, but one does not exercise the usual benefits associated with ownership, such as possession, until the future interest becomes a present interest.

Thus, where O conveys "to A for life, then to B and his heirs," A has a present interest, which gives her an immediate right to enjoy the property, and a life estate, which gives her a right to enjoy the property until she dies and the estate terminates. B has a future interest, which gives him a right to enjoy the property starting at some point in the future, and a fee simple absolute, which gives him a right to enjoy the property forever. Obviously, B actually cannot enjoy the property after he dies, but his right to enjoy the property forever means that his heirs will receive his interest upon his death if he has not otherwise disposed of it. When A dies and her estate terminates, B's future interest transforms into a present interest. If B is alive at the time of A's death and has not otherwise disposed of his interest, B has an immediate right to enjoy the property. If B dies before A's death and has not otherwise disposed of his interest, B's future interest descends to his heirs by intestate succession and later, upon A's death, it becomes a present interest.

In the example above, B's future interest follows the *natural termination* of the preceding estate in A. The natural termination of an estate occurs only when it is a life estate or a fee tail. A fee simple absolute has the potential of infinite duration and cannot terminate naturally. For example, where O (owning land in fee simple absolute) conveys "to A for life, then to B and the heirs of his body," O conveys a present interest in a life estate to A, which is followed upon its natural termination by a future interest in a fee tail in B, which in turn is followed upon its natural termination by a future interest in a fee simple absolute retained by O, the grantor. Note that O's original present interest in fee simple absolute has been divided into three interests/estates. Since O did not specify someone to take his property after the natural termination of both A's life estate and B's fee tail, the rest of O's original property interest remains in O as a future interest in fee simple absolute. If A dies before B's line of issue runs out, her estate has reached the end of its duration and terminates naturally, while B's future interest transforms into a present interest. If B's line of issue runs out before A dies, B's estate has reached the end of its duration and terminates naturally, while A's present interest continues. When both A has died and B's line of issue has run out, the estates of both A and B have terminated naturally and O's future interest transforms into a present interest.

A future interest also may follow the *unnatural termination* of a preceding estate in a grantee. For example, where O conveys "to A for life, then to B and his heirs" and then A forfeits her life estate because of waste, B's future interest transforms into a present interest at that time. The forfeiture of A's life estate for waste is an unnatural termination because it occurs before the time of natural termination that is A's death.

Finally, a future interest may *shift* or *spring* from a preceding estate when the preceding estate is *cut short* by a condition subsequent. The future interest shifts from the preceding estate when the preceding estate is in a grantee; the future interest springs from the preceding estate when the preceding estate is in the grantor. For example, where O conveys "to A and his heirs, but if A divorces, then to B," B's future interest shifts from the preceding estate in A upon the happening of the condition subsequent of A's divorce which cuts short A's preceding estate. Where O conveys "to B if and when A divorces," B's future interest springs from the preceding estate in O upon the happening of the condition subsequent of A's divorce which cuts short O's preceding estate. Note that O owns the preceding estate because O's conveyance has not designated anyone to take a present interest and therefore the present interest remains in O.

A future interest may be part of a number of interests, all of which shift or spring from a preceding estate cut short by a condition subsequent. For example, where O conveys "to A and her heirs, but if A divorces, then to B for life and then to C," O conveys a present interest to A in fee simple subject to executory limitation, a future interest (prepared to shift from A's estate upon the happening of the condition subsequent of A's divorce) to B in a life estate, and a future interest (which, along with the future interest in B, is prepared to shift from A's estate upon A's divorce) to C in a fee simple absolute. Note that from the original present interest in fee simple absolute, O has created two separate lines of conveyances. There is no natural connection between the estate of A and the estates of B and C. If the condition subsequent occurs (that is, A divorces), A's estate is cut short and replaced by the estates of B and C. Then B would have a present interest in a life estate and C would have a future interest in a fee simple absolute.

Likewise, where O conveys "to A for life, then to B and his heirs as long as B does not divorce, but if B divorces, then to C for life and then to D," O conveys a present interest to A in a life estate, a future interest (following the termination of A's life estate) to B in fee simple subject to executory limitation, a future interest (prepared to shift from B's estate upon the happening of the condition subsequent of B's divorce) to C in a life estate, and a future interest (which, along with the future interest in C, is prepared to shift from B's estate upon A's divorce) to D in fee simple absolute. Note again that from the original present interest in fee simple absolute, O has created two separate lines of conveyances. There is no natural connection between the estates of A and B and the estates of C and D. However, if the condition subsequent occurs (that is, A divorces), B's estate is cut short and replaced by the estates of C and D. Then the ownerships in the land would be naturally connected. A would continue to hold a present interest in a life estate, C would have a future interest (following the termination of A's life estate) in a life estate, and D would have a future interest (following the termination of A's life estate and C's life estate) in a fee simple absolute.

An example of a springing future interest is where O conveys "to A for life, then one year later to B for life, then to C." In this conveyance O gives a present interest to A in a life estate, retains a future interest (following A's life estate) in fee simple subject to executory limitation, gives a future interest (which springs from the grantor's estate) to B in a life estate, and gives a future interest (which, along with B's future interest, springs from the grantor's estate) to C in fee simple absolute. When A dies, A's life estate terminates naturally and O's future interest becomes a present interest. One year after A dies, the condition subsequent of the passage of one year has occurred to sever O's fee simple. At this point the ownerships in the land are a present interest in B in a life estate and a future interest in C in fee simple absolute.

1. Future Interests in the Grantor

Future interests in the grantor are called reversionary interests. They are interests in the grantor's original estate retained by the grantor. They are:

(1) **possibility of reverter,** which *always* shifts from an estate determinable:

> "to A and her heirs as long as A does not divorce, then to O, the original grantor";

(2) **right of reentry** or **power of termination,** which *always* shifts from an estate subject to condition subsequent:

> "to A and her heirs, but if A divorces, then to O, the original grantor";

(3) **reversion,** which stands ready to take at any time the preceding estates in grantees terminate other than by a condition subsequent. (Note that a reversion coupled with a possibility of reverter are both considered together as a reversion.);

(4) **reversionary interest** (so called for lack of a more specific term), which follows an executory interest and has the potential of becoming a possibility of reverter, a right of reentry or a reversion:

> "to A and her heirs as long as A does not divorce, then to B for life, then to O, the original grantor" or "to A and her heirs, but if A divorces, then to B for life, then to O, the original grantor."

2. Future Interests in a Grantee

Future interests in a grantee are:

(1) *remainder,* which follows the natural termination of life estate(s) and/or fee tail(s) if all conditions precedent are satisfied (although, if all conditions precedent are satisfied, the remainder may follow these estates if and when they are sooner cut short by a condition subsequent or they terminate unnaturally):

> "to *A* for life, then to *B* and the heirs of his body, then to *C* if *C* gets married" (*B* has a remainder that follows the termination of *A*'s life estate; *C* has a remainder that follows the termination of both *A*'s life estate and *B*'s fee tail if the condition precedent of *C*'s marriage is satisfied.),

> "to *A* for life as long as *A* does not divorce, then to *B*" (*B* has a remainder that follows the termination of *A*'s life estate unless *A*'s life estate is cut short by the condition subsequent of *A*'s divorce, in which case *B*'s remainder takes upon the event of *A*'s divorce.);

(2) *executory interest,* which is everything else, that is, one that shifts or springs from a preceding estate cut short by a condition subsequent (or is part of a number of interests, all of which together shift or spring from a preceding estate cut short by a condition subsequent and each of which is called an executory interest):

> "to *A* and her heirs, but if *A* divorces, then to *B* for life, then to *C* and the heirs of his body, then to *D*" (*B* has an executory interest in a life estate, *C* has an executory interest in a fee tail, and *D* has an executory interest in a fee simple absolute. These executory interests shift from *A*'s fee simple subject to executory limitation.),

> "to *A* for life, then one year later to *B*" (*B* has an executory interest in a fee simple absolute. This executory interest springs from *O*'s fee simple subject to executory limitation.).

D.   SUBCATEGORIES OF REMAINDERS

1. Contingent Remainder

A *remainder* may be *contingent* or *vested*. A *contingent remainder* is a remainder that is subject to a condition precedent. In other words, it is a remainder (1) in an unborn person, (2) in an unascertained person, or (3) subject to some other condition precedent. The *condition precedent* is a condition that must occur before the remainder will be allowed to take following the termination of the preceding life estate(s) and/or fee tail(s). For example, where O conveys "to A for life, then to B if B gets married," B has a contingent remainder. The condition precedent is B's marriage. If B gets married before A dies, then B's remainder will take upon A's death by becoming a present interest. If B has not married on or before A dies, then B's remainder will not be permitted to take upon A's death.

Conditions precedent must be distinguished from conditions subsequent. A condition precedent is one that must occur before a future interest (such as a contingent remainder) will be allowed to take; a condition subsequent is one whose occurrence will cause an estate to end (and thus allow a succeeding future interest such as an executory interest or a reversionary interest to take). It is helpful to examine three examples:

"to A for life, then to B if B gets married" (The condition precedent of B's marriage must occur if B's remainder is to take as a present interest upon the termination of A's life estate. Note that the occurrence of the condition precedent does not cut short A's life estate; it merely enables B's remainder to take upon the termination of A's life estate.),

"to A and her heirs, but if A divorces, then to B" (The condition subsequent of A's divorce cuts short A's estate in fee simple subject to executory limitation and allows B's executory interest to take immediately as a present interest. The condition of A's divorce may also be called a condition precedent that must occur if B's executory interest is to take as a present interest, but this aspect of the condition is rarely discussed since it serves no useful purpose of analysis.),

"to A and her heirs, as long as A does not divorce, then to O, the original grantor" (The condition subsequent of A's divorce cuts short A's estate in fee simple determinable and allows O's possibility of reverter to take immediately as a present interest. The condition of A's divorce may also be called a condition precedent that must occur if O's possibility of reverter is to take as a present interest, but again this aspect of the condition is rarely discussed.).

Alternative contingent remainders occur when two contingent remainders follow an estate and the condition precedent for one is the opposite of the condition precedent for the other. For example, where O conveys "to A for life, then to B if A divorces, and to C if A does not divorce," B and C have alternative contingent remainders. If A divorces, then B's remainder becomes a present interest upon A's death (C's remainder is destroyed by failure of the condition precedent); if A does not divorce, then C's remainder becomes a present interest upon A's death (B's remainder is destroyed by failure of the condition precedent).

When a remainder is given to a person "or" her children, the word "or" is usually construed as disjunctive, giving alternative contingent remainders to the person and to her children. The condition precedent is survivorship. For example, where O conveys "to A for life, then to B or her children," the condition precedent to B's contingent remainder is B's survivorship of A's death; the condition precedent to the children's contingent remainder is the failure of B to survive A. The same analysis would apply if the conveyance read "to B or her heirs" or "to B or her issue."

2. *Vested Remainder*

A *vested remainder* is a remainder that stands ready to take without contingency at any time the preceding estates terminate (or are sooner cut short). A contingent remainder becomes vested when its condition precedent (or conditions precedent) is satisfied. When its condition precedent is satisfied before the preceding estates terminate, the contingent remainder becomes a vested remainder. When its condition precedent is satisfied at the same time that the preceding estates terminate, the contingent remainder becomes a present interest, which is said to be vested in possession. There are three types of vested remainder:

(1) *indefeasibly vested* (usually this terminology is not used and the remainder is merely called *vested*), which means that its estate is absolute:

"to *A* for life, then to *B*";

(2) *vested subject to (complete) divestment,* which means that its estate is determinable, subject to condition subsequent or subject to executory limitation:

"to *A* for life, then to *B* and her heirs, but if *B* divorces, then to *C*";

(3) *vested subject to open* or *vested subject to partial divestment,* which means that its grantee (who is born, ascertained, and has an interest that is not subject to a condition precedent) may be joined by one or more other persons to share equally in the interest:

"to *A* for life, then to the children of *B*" (At the time of the conveyance, *B* is alive and has two children, *X* and *Y*. *X* and *Y* both share a vested remainder subject to open.)

Vested remainders subject to open are described more thoroughly in the next chapter. For the moment it is helpful to review the classification scheme that has been discussed so far to identify interests and estates in land.

E.   SUMMARY: DICHOTOMOUS KEY FOR IDENTIFICATION PROCEDURE

1. For each person who takes an estate in Blackacre under a conveyance you must ask what is his *interest* and what is his *estate* (in that order). You must always *separate* between these two!
2. Under *interest,* is it *present* or *future*? If it is present, there is nothing further to ask about the interest.
3. Under *future interest,* is it in the *grantor* or a *grantee*?

C. life estate
D. life estate pur autre vie
E. life estate determinable
F. life estate subject to condition subsequent
G. life estate subject to executory limitation
H. fee tail
I. fee tail determinable
J. fee tail subject to condition subsequent
K. fee tail subject to executory limitation
L. fee simple absolute
M. fee simple determinable
N. fee simple subject to condition subsequent
O. fee simple subject to executory limitation
P. none
Q. none of the above is correct

M

Problems

O conveys Blackacre to Arthur and his heirs.

1. What is Arthur's estate? *L FEE SIMPLE ABSOLUTE*
2. What is the estate of Arthur's heirs? *P - NONE*

O conveys Blackacre to Arthur for life. Arthur then conveys his interest to Barbara.

3. What is Barbara's estate? *D - LIFE ESTATE PUR AUTRE VIE*

O conveys to *A* for life, then one day later to *C* and his heirs.

4. What is *C*'s interest? *B = EXECUTORY INTEREST*

O conveys to *A* and the heirs of his body, but if the old oak tree falls, *O* may enter and take the property as of his former estate.

5. What is *A*'s estate? *J - FEE TAIL SUBJECT TO CONDITION SUBSEQUENT*
6. What is *O*'s interest? *E - RIGHT OF REENTRY*

O conveys to *A* for life, then to *B* and her heirs, but if *A* divorces, then, upon the divorce, to *C*.

7. What is *A*'s estate? *E - LIFE ESTATE DETERMINABLE*
8. What is *C*'s estate? *G - LIFE ESTATE SUBJECT TO EXECUTORY LIMITATION*

O conveys to *A* and the heirs of her body, then to *B*, with both estates to continue only as long as *C* does not get married.

9. What is *A*'s estate? *I - FEE TAIL DETERMINABLE*
10. What is *B*'s interest? *I - NONE ABOVE (SHLD BE VESTED REMAINDER SUBJECT TO DIVESTMENT.*
11. What is *O*'s interest? *G - POSSIBILITY OF REVERTER*

O conveys to Arthur and his heirs, but if Arthur uses the property for agricultural purposes, to Bob and the heirs of his body.

12. What is Arthur's estate? *O - FEE SIMPLE SUBJECT TO EXECUTOR*
13. What is Bob's interest? *- B - EXECUTORY INTEREST LIMITATION*

O conveys to *A* for ten years.

14. What is *A*'s estate? *A - TERM OF YEARS*

O conveys to John and his heirs until Abby graduates from law school, then to David and his heirs.

15. What is John's estate? *B - TERMS OF YEARS DETERMINABLE*

O conveys to *A* for life, then to *B* if *B* survives *A*, then to *C* if *B* does not survive *A*.

16. What is *C*'s interest? *- EXECUTORY INTEREST*

O conveys to *A* to have and to hold during the life of *B*.

17. What is *A*'s estate? *LIFE ESTATE PUR AUTRE VIE*

O conveys to *A* for 49 years or until the land lies fallow, whichever is first.

18. What is *A*'s estate? *TERM OF YEARS*

O conveys to *A* and the heirs of his body, then to *B* for life if *B* gets married.

19. What is *A*'s interest? *- PRESENT*
20. What is *A*'s estate? *- FEE TAIL*
21. What is *B*'s estate? *- CONTINGENT REMAINDER LIFE ESTATE*

O conveys Blackacre to *A* for life, then to *B* for life, but if Blackacre is not maintained as a farm, then it shall revert to *O* upon *O*'s reentry.

22. What is *B*'s estate? *- LIFE ESTATE SUBJECT TO CONDITION SUB*
23. What is *O*'s interest? *- RIGHT OF RE-ENTRY*

O conveys to *A* and her heirs, but if *B* gets married, then, upon his marriage, to *B* for life, then to *C* and his heirs.

24. What is *B*'s interest? *EXECUTORY INTEREST LIFE ESTATE*
25. What is *C*'s interest? *FEE SIMPLE SUBJECT TO EXECUTORY INTEREST*

O conveys to *A* for life, then to *B* if *B* gets married, and if *B* does not have a son by the time of *A*'s death, then to *C*. *B* has never been married or had children.

26. What is *B*'s interest? *- CONTINGENT R*
27. What is *C*'s interest?

O conveys to *A* for life, then, if *B* gets married, to *B* and his heirs as long as *B* stays married. *B* has never married.

    28.   What is *B*'s interest?

O conveys to *A* for life, then to *B* and her heirs if *B* attends *A*'s funeral.

    29.   What is *B*'s interest?

O conveys to *A* and the heirs of his body by his wife, *B*.

    30.   What is *A*'s estate?

O conveys to *A* for life or until he has a son.

    31.   What is *A*'s interest?
    32.   What is *O*'s interest?

O conveys to *A* for life, then to *B* and his heirs, then to *C* or her heirs.

    33.   What is the interest in *B*'s heirs?
    34.   What is the interest in *C*'s heirs?

O conveys to *A* and her heirs, as long as *A* puts a rose each year on the grave of *O*'s deceased grandmother until *A*'s death, otherwise to *B* for life.

    35.   What is *A*'s estate?
    36.   What is *O*'s interest?

O conveys to *A* for life, but if *A* gets married, then *O* shall have the right to reenter and possess the property as of his former estate.

    37.   What is *O*'s interest?

O conveys to *A* and her heirs, but if *A* does not enter law school, then the property shall revert to *O*.

    38.   What is *A*'s estate?

O conveys to *A* and his heirs until *A* gets married, then to *B* and the heirs of his body, but if *B* gets married, then to *C*.

    39.   What is *B*'s estate?

O conveys to *A* for life, then to *B* and his issue, then to *C* and his heirs if *C* gets married, but if *C* does not get married, then to *D* as long as the old oak tree remains standing.

    40.   What is *D*'s interest?

O conveys to *A* for life, then to *B* and her heirs on condition that if the oak tree on the property does not remain standing, *O* shall have the right to retake the property as of his former estate.

41. What is *O*'s interest?

O conveys to *A* for life, then to *B* and his issue, then to *C*'s children. *C* is alive and has one child, *X*, at the time of the conveyance.

42. What is *B*'s estate?
43. What is the estate of *B*'s issue?
44. What is the interest of *X*?

O, owning a present interest in a fee tail, conveys all her interest to *A*.

45. In effect, what is *A*'s estate?

O conveys to *A* and the heirs of her body, then to *B* for life if *B* gets married, then one day later to *C*.

46. What is *B*'s interest?
47. What is *O*'s interest?
48. What is *C*'s interest?

O, owning a vested remainder in a life estate, conveys to *A* and her heirs, but if *A* divorces, then to *B*.

49. What is *A*'s interest?
50. What is *B*'s interest?

Answers

1. *L. Fee simple absolute.* "To Arthur" are words of purchase.
2. *P. None.* "And his heirs" are words of limitation.
3. *D. Life estate pur autre vie.* *O* conveys a life estate to Arthur. Arthur's estate when it is transferred to Barbara continues to be measured by Arthur's life and to be followed by *O*'s reversion.
4. *B. Executory interest* springing after a reversion. *A* takes a life estate, and *O* retains a reversion in fee simple subject to executory limitation.
5. *J. Fee tail subject to condition subsequent.* The words of limitation for the fee tail estate are "and the heirs of his body." The condition subsequent uses words of condition ("but if"). If words of duration had been used without the entry language, *A* would have had a fee tail determinable.
6. *J. None of the above is correct.* *O*'s reversion is coupled with a right of reentry. Since the latter requires the exercise of an option to enter by *O*, it is appropriate to call *O*'s interest a reversion coupled with a right of reentry (rather than just a reversion).
7. *G. Life estate subject to executory limitation.* The condition subsequent (*A*'s divorce) cuts short both *A*'s life estate subject to executory limitation and *B*'s fee simple subject to executory limitation.
8. *L. Fee simple absolute.*
9. *I. Fee tail determinable.* The condition subsequent uses words of duration ("as long as"), and there is no grantee designated to take upon the happening of the condition subsequent.

10. *F. Vested remainder* in fee simple determinable. *B's* interest stands ready to follow the natural termination of the preceding fee tail estate in *A* without any condition precedent that needs to be satisfied for it to take.

11. *G. Possibility of reverter*. When there is no grantee designated to take upon the happening of a condition subsequent that is durational rather than conditional, the grantor retains a possibility of reverter. When the condition subsequent occurs, it will cut short *A's* fee tail determinable and *B's* fee simple determinable, and the possibility of reverter will transform into a present interest in *O*.

12. *O. Fee simple subject to executory limitation*. It is followed by an interest in a grantee.

13. *B. Executory interest* in fee tail. *O* has a reversion in fee simple absolute.

14. *A. Term of years*. *O* retains a present interest in fee simple absolute. In essence, *O* as landlord has given a lease to *A* as tenant.

15. *O. Fee simple subject to executory limitation*. It does not matter whether words of condition or words of duration are used in the condition subsequent.

16. *D. Contingent remainder*. *B* and *C* have alternative contingent remainders because each interest is accompanied by a condition that is treated as a condition precedent.

17. *D. Life estate pur autre vie*. *B's* life measures the duration of *A's* estate. If *A* dies without transfering her estate, *A's* heirs inherit the estate, which continues to last until the death of *B*.

18. *B. Term of years determinable*. The duration of the estate is limited to 49 years and may be terminated before that time by a condition ("until the land lies fallow"). It is a nonfreehold estate. *O* retains a reversion in fee simple absolute subject to this term of years.

19. *A. Present interest.*

20. *H. Fee tail.*

21. *C. Life estate*. *B* has a contingent remainder in a life estate. The condition "if *B* gets married" is a condition precedent to *B's* interest; it is not a condition subsequent to *A's* estate nor to *B's* estate. *O* retains a reversion in fee simple absolute.

22. *F. Life estate subject to condition subsequent*. The condition subsequent is the failure to maintain Blackacre as a farm.

23. *J. None of the above is correct*. *O* has a right of reentry ready to cut short both life estates subject to condition subsequent, and *O* also has a reversion ready to follow the natural termination of both life estates subject to condition subsequent. Since the former requires the exercise of an option to enter by *O*, it is appropriate to call *O's* interest a reversion coupled with a right of reentry (rather than just a reversion).

24. *B. Executory interest* in a life estate. The condition of *B's* getting married is precedent to *B's* interest and subsequent to *A's* fee simple estate. It cuts off *A's* estate if it occurs. Therefore, both *B* and *C* have executory interests. (If the condition happens, *B* gets

a present interest in a life estate and *C*'s executory interest transforms into a vested remainder in fee simple absolute.)

25. *B.   Executory interest.* *C*'s executory interest and *B*'s executory interest together shift from *A*'s fee simple subject to executory limitation upon the happening of the condition subsequent (*B*'s marriage).

26. *D.   Contingent remainder* in fee simple absolute. The condition precedent is *B*'s marriage. *O* has a reversion following *A*'s present interest in a life estate.

27. *D.   Contingent remainder* in fee simple absolute. The condition precedent is *B*'s not having a son by the time of *A*'s death. (If *B* were to get married, *B* would have a vested remainder in fee simple subject to executory limitation and *C* would have an executory interest in fee simple absolute. If *A* were then to die while *B* remains childless, the condition subsequent (*B*'s not having a son by the time of *A*'s death) would cut short *B*'s estate and *C* would have a present interest in fee simple absolute.)

28. *D.   Contingent remainder* in fee simple determinable. The condition "if *B* gets married" is precedent to *B*'s remainder. *O* has a reversion and a possibility of reverter. (If *B* were to get married, he would have a vested remainder in fee simple determinable followed by a possibility of reverter in *O*.) The condition "as long as *B* stays married" is subsequent to *B*'s fee simple estate and precedent to *O*'s possibility of reverter.

29. *B.   Executory interest* in fee simple absolute. *A* has a life estate, *O* has a reversion between the end of *A*'s life estate and *A*'s funeral. *B* has an executory interest that becomes a present interest if he satisfies the condition (attending *A*'s funeral).

30. *H.   Fee tail.* More specifically, *A* has a fee tail special. It is limited to descent from a particular marriage. *O* has a reversion in fee simple absolute.

31. *E.   Life estate determinable.* The condition subsequent is *A*'s having a son.

32. *C.   Reversion* in fee simple absolute. *O* has a possibility of reverter to follow the life estate determinable in *A* if the condition subsequent occurs, but *O* also has a reversion. Therefore, we call *O*'s interest simply a reversion.

33. *I.   None.* "And his heirs" are words of limitation and give no interest to *B*'s heirs.

34. *D.   Contingent remainder.* The word "or" is construed as disjunctive, and both *C* and *C*'s heirs are given alternative contingent remainders. The condition precedent to *C*'s interest is her survivorship of *A* and *B*. The condition precedent to *C*'s heirs interest is the failure of *C* to survive *A* and *B*.

35. *O.   Fee simple subject to executory limitation.* The condition subsequent is *A*'s failure to put a rose on *O*'s grandmother's grave each year until *A*'s death. The condition is also precedent to *B*'s executory interest in a life estate, thus making *A*'s estate "subject to executory limitation."

36. *J.   None of the above is correct.* *O* retains an interest following *B*'s life estate. It is neither a possibility of reverter nor a right of

reentry because it does not follow immediately upon the cutting short of *A*'s estate. For lack of a better term, this interest is called merely a reversionary interest in *O*. If *B* dies before *A* and the condition subsequent has not yet occurred, then *O*'s interest becomes a possibility of reverter. If the condition subsequent occurs before *B* dies, then *B* takes a present interest in a life estate and *O*'s interest is transformed into a reversion.

37. *J. None of the above is correct. O* has a reversion plus right of reentry. *A* has a life estate subject to condition subsequent. The interest in the grantor is more than a reversion. The right of reentry does not become effective automatically, but only at the will of the grantor. Therefore, the interest is best described in its two parts.

38. *N. Fee simple subject to condition subsequent.* The condition subsequent is introduced by words of condition indicating an intent to create a right of reentry (power of termination) in the grantor, *O*.

39. *K. Fee tail subject to executory limitation. A* has a fee simple subject to executory limitation. *B*'s executory interest is subject to the condition subsequent of *B*'s marriage. *C* has an executory interest in fee simple absolute. *O* has a reversionary interest following *B*'s fee tail.

40. *D. Contingent remainder* in fee simple determinable. *A* has a present interest in a life estate. *B* has a vested remainder in fee tail. *C* has a contingent remainder in fee simple absolute. *D*'s remainder is an alternative contingent remainder. *O* retains a reversion following *B*'s fee tail and a possibility of reverter following *D*'s fee simple determinable.

41. *E. Right of reentry* following *B*'s vested remainder in fee simple subject to condition subsequent. *B*'s interest is cut short upon the happening of the condition and the exercise by *O* of his right of reentry.

42. *H. Fee tail.* "And his issue" are words of limitation for a fee tail estate.

43. *P. None.* "And his issue" are words of limitation for a fee tail estate.

44. *H. Vested remainder subject to open. X*'s interest is vested because it is not subject to any condition precedent. However, it is an interest that may be shared with other children born to *C*.

45. *D. Life estate pur autre vie. A* does not have her own fee tail because it is only when *O* dies that the fee tail will pass on to issue, and it will be *O*'s issue who will take it. *A* has *O*'s fee tail estate until *O*'s death. In effect this gives *A* a life estate for the life of *O*.

46. *D. Contingent remainder* in a life estate. The condition precedent is *B*'s marriage.

47. *C. Reversion* in fee simple subject to executory limitation. If *B*'s marriage does not occur, *B*'s contingent remainder will not take, and *O*'s reversion will become a present interest at the end of *A*'s fee tail (when *A*'s line of descendants runs out). On the other hand, if *B* gets married before the death of the last of *A*'s descen-

dants, *B*'s contingent remainder becomes a vested remainder and eventually may become a present interest upon the termination of *A*'s fee tail (if *B* survives the termination of *A*'s fee tail). In either case, *C*'s executory interest becomes a present interest (by cutting short *O*'s fee simple subject to executory limitation) one day after *O*'s reversion becomes a present interest.

48. *B.   Executory interest* in fee simple absolute.

49. *F.   Vested remainder* in a life estate pur autre vie subject to executory limitation. *A* receives part of *O*'s vested remainder in a life estate; it has an added condition subsequent which is *A*'s divorce. Thus, *A*'s estate will end either on the death of *O* or on *A*'s divorce, whichever occurs first.

50. *J.   None of the above is correct. B* has part of *O*'s vested remainder, but it is not the first part. Therefore, it is inappropriate to call *B*'s interest a vested remainder. *B*'s interest and estate may be called an executory interest in a life estate pur autre vie within a vested remainder.

2

Class Interests

A. INCLUSION

All the people who are designated to share in an interest are considered a *class. A* class consists of a group, such as children, nephews, or parents. It may be a group within a group, such as grandchildren by one's oldest daughter.

A person becomes a member of a class at the moment of conception, as long as that person is later born alive. Thus, where O conveys "to A's children" at a time when A is pregnant with twins and has one child, X, who is already born, the members of the class at the time of conveyance are the two twins (as long as they are later born alive) and X. If, six months later, one of the twins is born alive and the other dies before birth, then the twin that is born alive continues to be considered a member of the class from the time of the conveyance, while the twin that dies before birth is considered never to have been a member of the class.

In determining the members of a class designated in a conveyance, one should be careful to distinguish the definition of a class from a condition precedent to the vesting or distribution of an interest of a class member. Although the literature on this subject is scanty, the cases seem to indicate that a characteristic of a class member, such as filial relationship or sex, defines the class, while an event, such as birth or the attainment of a certain age, poses a condition precedent to the vesting or distribution of a class member's interest. In the example above, the twin that is later born alive must satisfy the condition precedent of birth before her interest will become vested. At the time of the conveyance, both the child that is born and the twin that is later born alive are members of the class, but the child that is born has a vested present interest and the twin that is later born alive has an executory interest until she is born.

In this way the class will hold two interests when one is vested and the other is contingent. In the example above, the vested interest is held by X, the child that is born at the time of the conveyance. X has a "present interest subject to open" to let in other members of the class who may be born after the conveyance. More exactly, X has a present interest subject to open in a fee simple subject to executory limitation. The condition subsequent that provides the executory limitation only partially cuts short the vested interest when it happens. The condition subsequent is the birth of any member of the class so that the newly born member takes a share in the vested estate and cuts down proportionally, but never eliminates, the shares of the members already holding the vested estate. The contingent interest, held by the child that is not born at the time of the conveyance but will be born later, is an executory interest in a fee simple absolute. When the child is born, the executory interest transforms into the present interest already held by X, and both X and the newly born child share the present interest together.

The distinction between that which defines a class and that which is a condition precedent to the vesting or to the distribution of an interest of a class member may be illustrated by another example. Where O conveys "to the children of B who are female and who reach the age of 21," the class is the daughters of B, *not* the daughters of B who are 21 and older. At the time of this conveyance the daughters of B who are 21 and older are members of the class and hold a vested present interest subject to open in a fee simple subject to executory limitation. The daughters of B who are conceived (later to be born alive) and under age 21 are members of the class, but they must satisfy the condition precedent of reaching age 21 before their interest will become vested. They have an executory interest in a fee simple absolute. The daughters of B who are not yet conceived at the time of the conveyance are not members of the class. When they are conceived, if the class is still open to receiving members under the rules of exclusion described below, they become members of the class at the point of conception if they are later born alive.

This distinction between characteristics and events applies also to the conveyance of a future interest in a class. For example, where O conveys "to A for life, then to the children of B," the children of B, as a class, are given a remainder following A's life estate. If no children of B have yet been conceived, there are no members of the class at the time of the conveyance, but the children of B are said to have a contingent remainder in fee simple absolute. If a child of B is conceived (later to be born alive), that child becomes a member of the class of B's children at the time of conception, but this child in gestation still holds the contingent remainder in a fee simple absolute. When the child is born, she satisfies the condition precedent of birth and her contingent remainder becomes a vested remainder subject to open in a fee simple subject to executory limitation. The interest of the other children who are not yet born is transformed from a contingent remainder to an executory interest in a fee simple absolute. The condition subsequent that stands ready to cut short partially the estate of the child who is now born (that is, to open the vested remainder of the child who is now born) is the birth of any other child to B. Upon the birth of another child, that child's share in the executory interest transforms into a share in the vested remainder subject to open that is held by the first child who was born, while the rest of the children who are not yet born continue to hold the executory interest.

Note one aberration from the logic of these rules that originates from a case decided by the House of Lords in the seventeenth century: In a conveyance "to A for life, remainder to A's first son and his heirs," if A has a son conceived but not born at the termination of A's life estate and the son is later born alive, the law creates the fiction that the child is considered born at the moment of A's death. The purpose of this fiction is to avoid a reversion in the grantor by giving the child in gestation a vested present interest. Thus, in a conveyance "to A's children," if A's first child is conceived at the time of the conveyance (later to be born alive), the child is considered born at the moment of the conveyance. Also, in a conveyance "to A for life, then to the children of B," if B's first child is conceived at the time of A's death (later to be born alive), the child is considered born at the moment of A's death. The fiction of birth creates a vested interest in the child in gestation; however, distribution of the child's interest most likely will be postponed until birth.

B. EXCLUSION

1. Class Closing Rules

Not all people in a class are entitled to become "members" of the class. A class "opens" to accept new members upon their conception (if they are later born alive), and a class may also "close" to prevent new people in the class from becoming members. Thus, a class may be defined as the children of A, and, if the class closes after two children are born to A, then any children conceived by A after the class closes are not members of the class and do not take any share with the members of the class. The people in a class must be conceived before the class closes if they are to be qualified as members of the class.

A class "closes," so that no more people may be admitted to the class, upon the happening of one of two events, *whichever is sooner*:

(1) *natural closing*: when there are no more members who can join the class, or

(2) *time determined by rule of convenience*: when the time designated in the conveyance for distribution has arrived, and at that time there exists some member of the class (or one who has inherited, bought, or otherwise received the interest of some member of the class) to take distribution.

Natural closing: The first event closes the class naturally. Thus, where O conveys "to A for life, then one year later to the children of B," the class of B's children will close naturally if and when B dies before the passage of one year from A's death, since B can have no more children. Note that the class is not considered naturally closed before B's death even if B reaches the ripe old age of 110 and is physically incapable of having children, because the law conclusively presumes a fiction, that is, that any person who is alive is capable of having children.

Time determined by rule of convenience: The second event closes the class at a time when a member (or someone holding the interest of a member) is entitled to distribution. The closing of the class determines the maximum membership of the class because any person who is not a member at that time will be barred from membership. By setting the maximum membership, the closing of the class determines the minimum share of each class member. This determination is a matter of convenience to the member who has become, and those members who will become, entitled to distribution. They know at least the minimum amount of their share. It will never decrease, although it may grow if the class decreases for failure of a member to satisfy a condition precedent.

One important aspect of the rule of convenience is that the class will not close under this rule if a member of the class comes into existence (and thus becomes entitled to distribution) after the time for distribution has passed. At least one class member (or a person holding the interest of a class member) must be in existence at the time designated in the conveyance for distribution. The time designated in the conveyance for distribution is the time distribution would take place if there were a member of the class in existence. Thus, in the conveyance "to *A*'s children" the time for distribution is the time of conveyance; in the conveyance "to *A*'s children who reach 15" the time for distribution is the time *A*'s first child reaches 15; and in the conveyance "to *A* for life, then one year later to the children of *B*" the time for distribution is the time one year has passed after *A*'s death. When the time for distribution has arrived, if there is no class member (or person holding the interest of a class member) in existence, the rule of convenience will not apply. Note that in the conveyances "to *A*'s children" and "to *A* for life, then one year later to the children of *B*" it is possible for the time for distribution to take place without any class members in existence, but in the conveyance "to *A*'s children who reach 15" it is not possible for the time for distribution to take place unless a class member is in existence. Note also that existence starts from the point of conception, as long as the conceived person is later born alive. One final note: The rule of convenience is a rule of construction and will yield to a contrary intent in the grantor.

2. Four Examples

Since the combination of class membership definition, conditions precedent to vesting, and class closing rules often gives rise to confusion, the discussion above is expanded below with four examples.

(1) Where *O* conveys "to *A*'s children" and there are children alive at the time of the conveyance, the class closes immediately under the rule of convenience and includes only those children. If *A* has two children, *F* and *G*, at the time of the conveyance, these children have a present interest in fee simple absolute. No other children conceived after the conveyance will become members of the class.

If there are no children alive at the time of the conveyance, the class remains open until *A*'s death (natural closing), and the rule of convenience does not apply. *O* retains a present interest in fee simple subject to executory limitation and *A*'s unborn children have an executory interest in fee simple absolute. If *A* then bears a child, *P*, *P* takes a present interest subject to open in fee simple absolute, divesting *O*'s present interest in the process. *A*'s unborn children continue to have an executory interest. If *A* then dies, the class closes and *P* has a present interest in fee simple absolute.

(2) Where *O* conveys "to the children of *A* who reach 21," the class is *A*'s children (*not A*'s children who reach 21). The class closes at the time of the earliest of the following events: the time *A* dies (natural closing), or the time a child of *A* reaches 21 if that happens for the first time after the conveyance (rule of convenience), or the time the conveyance becomes effective if a child of *A* reaches 21 before the conveyance (rule of convenience). When the class closes, all members who are born (or conceived, if later born alive) who have not yet reached 21 are entitled to a share when they do reach 21. All children conceived after the class closes (or conceived before but never born alive) are not members of the class.

O's conveyance in this case where one child, *W*, has reached 21 and other children, *X* and *Y*, are born but not yet 21, gives *W* a present interest subject to open and gives *X* and *Y* an executory interest. *X* and *Y* take a share with *W* in the present interest when they reach 21. Reaching 21 is a condition precedent to transforming the interest of each into a vested present interest and is a condition subsequent to *W*'s estate to the extent that *W*'s share will be decreased to admit the share of *X* and/or *Y*. Two years later, if *X* reaches 21 and *Y* dies before reaching 21 and *Z* is born, *X* takes a share in the ownership of *W*'s estate. *Y* is excluded for not satisfying the age contingency and *Z* is excluded for being conceived after the class closes.

(3) Where *O* conveys "to *X* for life, then one year later to *A*'s children" and *A* has two children, *G* and *H*, the ownerships are as follows: *X* has a present interest in a life estate, *O* has a reversion in fee simple subject to executory limitation, and *G* and *H* share an executory interest in fee simple absolute with *A*'s unborn children. The condition subsequent on *O*'s fee simple subject to executory limitation is the passage of one year after the termination of *X*'s life estate; this same condition is precedent to the vesting of the interest in *G* and *H*. The class closes upon the earlier of two events: *A*'s death (natural closing) or the passage of one year since the termination of *X*'s life estate (rule of convenience), because *A* has children (or at least a child of *A* was alive at or after *O*'s conveyance, so that someone holds the interest of a member of the class one year after the termination of *X*'s life estate).

If *A* does not have children at the time of this conveyance, then *X* has a present interest in a life estate, *O* has a reversion in fee simple subject to executory limitation, and *A*'s unborn children have an executory interest in fee simple absolute. There are two conditions subsequent on *O*'s estate: the passage of one year from the termination of *X*'s estate and the birth of a child to *A*. Both conditions must be realized before *O*'s reversion is divested. Furthermore, if *A* has not conceived children to create a member of the class by the time designated in the conveyance for distribution, that is, one year past the termination of *X*'s life estate, the rule of convenience does not apply and the class remains open until A's death, so that children born to A after the time for distribution become members.

(4) Where O conveys "to L for life, then one year later to such of A's children who reach 21" and A has no children, O conveys an executory interest in fee simple absolute to A's children as a class. L has a present interest in a life estate, and O retains a reversion in fee simple subject to executory limitation. O's estate will be cut short (another way of saying that O's reversion will be divested) when one year has passed from the termination of L's life estate and at least one child of A has been born and reached 21, or it will be cut short at the time that any child of A reaches 21 if that occurs for the first time more than one year after the termination of L's life estate. In either case the class will close under the rule of convenience (if it has not already closed naturally) by the presence of a 21-year-old child of A (or someone who holds the interest of a 21-year-old child of A) at or after the passage of one year from L's death. If the class closes under the rule of convenience, only members of the class at that time (or those who hold the interest of members of the class) will be permitted to be members and only those members who reach 21 will be permitted to take their shares. All children conceived after O's estate is cut short will not be a part of the class entitled to take and will take nothing.

Thus, if A's child, X, reaches 21 and one year has already passed since L died, or if X reaches 21 and then one year passes since L died, O's estate is cut short and X's executory interest becomes a present interest. If there is only one other child, Y, who has been conceived by this time, Y's interest remains executory. When Y reaches 21, Y joins X as a tenant in common sharing X's estate in fee simple absolute. If another child of A is conceived after O's estate is cut short, that child is not entitled to distribution.

In more precise terms for the purpose of classification of estates, if A has two children under age 21, X and Y, at the time of or after the conveyance, then X and Y have an executory interest in fee simple absolute. They are said to share their executory interest in fee simple absolute with the unborn children of A, even though the unborn children of A are not yet members of the class. Their executory interest stands ready to cut short O's fee simple upon the happening of two conditions subsequent to O's estate (one child reaching 21 and one year passage from the termination of L's life estate). The two conditions subsequent on O's fee simple are simultaneously conditions precedent to the executory interest held by X, Y, and the unborn children. When X reaches 21 and one year has passed since the termination of L's estate, if A has not conceived any other children, A's unborn children no longer have any interest because the class closes. Y continues to have an executory interest in fee simple absolute.

3. Distribution of Shares

Whenever a member of a class becomes entitled to distribution, that person may take his minimum proportionate share of the whole estate. For example, when O conveys "to the children of A who reach 21" and there are three children alive at the time of the conveyance (X, Y, and Z, ages 13, 18, and 22 respectively), the class is closed at the time of the conveyance and Z is entitled to a one-third share in the property in anticipation of the other two children's reaching 21. If Y dies before reaching 21, Z's share is increased to one-half. If X reaches 21, X is then entitled to the other half share. There is a problem in determining the minimum proportionate share in some cases. For example, when O conveys "to the children of A" and there are no children at the time of the conveyance, the class remains open until A's death. How much of the property does the first child of A take when she is born? It has been suggested that the first child takes the whole property subject to partial divestment when later children are born.

Problem Set II

The problems in this section ask for a description of an interest or an estate. The answers for interest are:

    A. present interest
    B. executory interest
    C. reversion
    D. contingent remainder
    E. right of reentry
    F. vested remainder
    G. possibility of reverter
    H. vested remainder subject to open
    I. none
    J. none of the above is correct

The answers for estate are:

    A. term of years
    B. term of years determinable
    C. life estate
    D. life estate pur autre vie
    E. life estate determinable
    F. life estate subject to condition subsequent
    G. life estate subject to executory limitation
    H. fee tail
    I. fee tail determinable
    J. fee tail subject to condition subsequent
    K. fee tail subject to executory limitation
    L. fee simple absolute
    M. fee simple determinable
    N. fee simple subject to condition subsequent
    O. fee simple subject to executory limitation
    P. none
    Q. none of the above is correct

Problems

O conveys to his children who reach 21 and their heirs. O has two children who are ages five and ten.

    51.   What is O's children's interest?

    52.   What is O's interest?

O conveys to A for life, then to B's children, but if no child of B reaches 21, then to C. B has one child, X, who is 15 years old at the time of the conveyance.

    53.   What is X's interest?

    54.   What is B's unborn children's interest?

O conveys to A for life, then to A's children who shall reach 21; and in case A shall become bankrupt, A's estate shall become void and shall vest in A's children who shall reach 21. None of A's children has reached 21.

    55.   What is the interest in A's born children?

    56.   What is A's estate?

O has no grandchildren living at his death. O devises Blackacre to his grandchildren.

    57.   What is the unborn grandchildren's interest?

O has two grandchildren, X and Y, living at her death. O devises Blackacre to her grandchildren.

    58.   What is the unborn grandchildren's interest?

O conveys to A for life, then to such of A's children as survive A. B is already born to A at the time of the conveyance.

    59.   What is B's interest?

    60.   What is O's interest?

O conveys to A and her issue, then to B or her children.

    61.   What is A's estate?

    62.   What is B's interest?

O conveys to A for life, then, if B goes to law school, to B and his issue, then to C's children. C has two children, X and Y, at the time of the conveyance.

    63.   What is B's estate?

    64.   What is X's estate?

O conveys to A's children who reach the age of twelve for the life of S, a stranger, then to B and his heirs. A has one two-year-old child, X.

65. What is *X*'s interest?
66. What is *B*'s interest?

O conveys to *A* for life, then to *A*'s children who shall reach 21; and in case *A* shall become bankrupt, *A*'s estate shall become void and shall vest in *A*'s children who shall reach 21. *A* has one child, *X*, who is 30 years old.

67. What is the interest in *X*?
68. What is *A*'s estate?

O has no grandchildren living at his death. *O* devises Blackacre to *A* for life, then to his grandchildren. Thirty years later, *O*'s first grandchild, *X*, is born.

69. What is *X*'s interest?
70. What is the unborn grandchildren's interest?

O has no grandchildren living at his death. *O* devises Blackacre to *A* for life, then to his grandchildren. Thirty years later *O*'s first grandchild, *X*, is born. The next year *O*'s second grandchild, *Y*, is conceived. Two months later *A* dies. Seven months later *Y* is born.

71. Upon *A*'s death, what is *Y*'s interest?
72. Upon *A*'s death, what is the interest of the unborn grandchildren other than *Y*?

O has no grandchildren living at his death. *O* devises Blackacre to *A* for life, then to his grandchildren. Thirty years later, *O*'s first grandchild, *X*, is born. Five years later *X* dies intestate, leaving his mother, *M*, as his only heir. Two years later *A* dies.

73. What is the unborn grandchildren's interest?

O has no grandchildren living at his death. *O* devises Blackacre to *A* for life, then one year later to his grandchildren. Five years later *A* dies. One year after *A*'s death there are still no grandchildren who have been conceived.

74. What is the unborn grandchildren's interest?

O conveys to *A* for life, then one year later to *B*'s children who reach 15 and their heirs. *B* has one child, *X*, at the time of the conveyance whose age is ten. Two years later *A* dies.

75. One year after *A*'s death what is *B*'s children's interest?
76. One year after *A*'s death what is *O*'s interest?
77. Four years after *A*'s death what is the interest of *B*'s children other than *X*?

O conveys to *A* and her issue, then to the children of *B*. At the time of the conveyance, *B* has one child. Two years later *B*'s child dies. Three years after the death of *B*'s child, *A* dies without ever having had children.

78.   What is *B*'s children's interest?
79.   What is *O*'s interest?

O conveys to *A* and her issue, then one year later to the children of *B*. At the time of the conveyance, neither *A* nor *B* has ever had children. Three years after the conveyance, *A* dies without ever having had children. Three years after *A*'s death, *B* has one child, *X*. Three years later, *B* has another child, *Y*, and dies shortly thereafter.

80.   What is *Y*'s estate?

O conveys to his children who reach 21 and their heirs. *O* has two children, *X*, who is 15 years old, and *Y*, who is 25 years old.

81.   What is *Y*'s interest?
82.   What is the interest of *O*'s children other than *X* and *Y*?

O conveys to *A* for life, then to his children who reach 21 and their heirs. *O* has two children, *X*, who is 15 years old, and *Y*, who is 25 years old. Two years later *A* dies. One month after *A*'s death, *Z*, *O*'s third child, is born. Two years after *A*'s death, *X* dies.

83.   What is *Y*'s interest?
84.   What is *Z*'s interest?

O conveys to the nieces of *A*. At the time of the conveyance *A* has no parents and one sister, *B*, who has never had children. Three years later *B* has a son, *X*. One year later *B* has a daughter, *Y*. Five years later *B* has another daughter, *Z*.

85.   What is *Z*'s interest?

O conveys to *A* for life, then to *B*'s grandchildren. At the time of the conveyance *B* is dead, but his two children, *R* and *S*, are alive. Two years after the conveyance, *A* dies while *R* is pregnant with *B*'s first grandchild. Two months later, *B*'s first grandchild, *X*, is born.

86.   At the time of *A*'s death, what is *X*'s interest?

O conveys to *A* for life, then to *B* and her issue, then to *C* for life, then to *D*'s children. Three years after the conveyance, *A*, *B*, *C*, and *D* all die in a plane crash. *A*, *B*, and *C* die childless. *D* had a child, *X*, who died one year before the plane crash and left a will that devised all his property to his mother, *M*. At the time of the plane crash, *D*'s wife, *M*, was pregnant but the news of the crash caused her to miscarry two weeks later.

87.   What is *M*'s estate?
88.   What is the interest in *D*'s unborn children?

O conveys to *A*'s children. Two years after the conveyance *A*, who is 40 years old, bears her first child, *X*. Seventy years later *A* celebrates her 110th birthday.

89.   What is the interest in *A*'s unborn children?

O devises to *A* and the heirs of her body, then to his grandchildren who reach the age of ten. At the time of the devise *O*'s grandchildren are: *X* who is five years old, *Y* who is seven years old, and *Z* who is eight years old. One year after the conveyance *Z* dies. Three years later *A* dies without ever having had children. At the time of *A*'s death, *O*'s fourth grandchild, *G*, is in gestation. One month later *H* is conceived. Two months later *G* is born on the same day that *Y* dies. One month later *G* and *X* die before either reaches the age of ten. Seven months later *H* is born.

90. At the time of the conveyance, what is *Y*'s interest?
91. At the time of *A*'s death, what is *G*'s interest?
92. At the time of *H*'s birth, what is *H*'s estate?
93. At the time of *H*'s birth, what is *O*'s interest?

O devises to *A*'s children for the life of the survivor. At the time of the conveyance, *A* has one child, *X*, who is one year old. Two years later *A* has a second child, *Y*. One year later *A* has a third child, *Z*. Five years later *X* and *Y* die in a car accident.

94. What is *Z*'s estate?

O devises to *O*'s grandchildren. At the time of the conveyance one grandchild, *R*, is in gestation. Two months later another grandchild, *S*, is in gestation. One month later *R* dies before birth. Eight months later *S* is born. Two years later a third grandchild, *T*, is born.

95. What is *S*'s estate?

O conveys to *A* and her issue, then one year later to the married children of *B*. One year after the conveyance *A* and *B* die, each leaving two adult children. *A*'s children, *F* and *G*, never have any children of their own and both live for another ten years when they both die of cancer. *B*'s children, *S* and *T*, are both single until *S* marries five years after the conveyance and *T* marries 15 years after the conveyance.

96. What is *T*'s interest?
97. What is *S*'s estate?

O conveys to *A*'s children, but if *X* goes to law school, then to *B*'s children. At the time of the conveyance *A* has no children. Two years later *A* bears triplets, *W*, *X*, and *Y*. Two years later *X* goes to law school. Three years later *X* graduates. One year later *B*'s first child, *F*, is born. Two years later *A*'s fourth child, *Z*, is born. Two years later *B*'s second child, *G*, is born.

98. What is *Z*'s interest?
99. What is *F*'s interest?
100. What is *G*'s interest?

Answers

51. *B.* *Executory interest* in fee simple absolute. *O*'s children are a class. The age requirement is a condition precedent on each of the children taking a vested interest. There is no life estate or fee

tail to support their interest as a remainder. Therefore, the children have an executory interest. When the first child reaches 21, the time for distribution has arrived and the class of children closes. All children conceived at that time (as long as they are or will be born alive) are a part of the class and entitled to take if and when each reaches 21. Thus, if the ten-year-old reaches 21 and at that time there are three children of *O*, the three children comprise the class. The oldest takes a present interest subject to open in fee simple subject to executory limitation (and actually receives one-third of the property), while the other two children continue to hold an executory interest in fee simple absolute. If one of the two younger children dies before reaching 21, he loses his interest and the first taker receives another one-sixth of the property. When the last child reaches 21, he shares the present interest in fee simple with his brother and receives the other half of the property.

52. A.   *Present interest* in fee simple subject to executory limitation. *O* retains the present interest in a freehold estate until the executory interest of the children transforms into a present interest.

53. H.   *Vested remainder subject to open* in a fee simple subject to executory interest. *X*'s fee simple is subject to two executory interests, one that would totally cut short *X*'s estate and the other that would partially cut it short. *C*'s executory interest in fee simple absolute would totally cut short *X*'s estate if no child of *B* reaches 21. The condition subsequent on *X*'s estate (which is also a condition precedent to the vesting of *C*'s interest) is the failure of any child of *B* to reach 21. *B*'s unborn children have the executory interest that would partially cut short *X*'s estate whenever a member of the class is born.

54. B.   *Executory interest* in fee simple absolute. *B*'s unborn children are admitted to *X*'s remainder as they are born. Membership in the class increases with every new conception (if followed later by live birth) until the class closes, that is, when *B* dies (natural closing) or *A*'s life estate terminates (rule of convenience), whichever is sooner.

55. J.   *None of the above is correct*. *A*'s children have a contingent remainder plus an executory interest. The remainder is contingent on the children reaching 21. It is accompanied by a reversion in *O* following *A*'s life estate. The executory interest is a separate interest in *A*'s children that cuts short *A*'s life estate (as well as divesting *O*'s reversion and destroying the contingent remainder in *A*'s children) if the two conditions subsequent (*A*'s becoming bankrupt and a child's becoming 21) occur. More exactly, *A* has a life estate determinable, subject to being cut short by the condition subsequent of *A*'s bankruptcy; *O* has a possibility of reverter in fee simple subject to executory limitation, with the estate subject to being cut short by the condition subsequent of a child of *A* becoming 21. If bankruptcy occurs before *A*'s child reaches 21, then upon bankruptcy *O*'s possibility of reverter will cut short *A*'s life estate to become a present

interest in fee simple subject to executory limitation, and upon *A*'s child becoming 21 *A*'s child's executory interest will cut short *O*'s estate to become a present interest. If bankruptcy occurs after *A*'s child reaches 21, then upon *A*'s child becoming 21 the executory interest in *A*'s child will cut short *O*'s estate and remain an executory interest, and upon bankruptcy it will cut short *A*'s life estate to become a present interest.

56.   *E.   Life estate determinable.* See problem 55 above.

57.   *B.   Executory interest* in fee simple absolute. *O*'s heirs, who inherit the undevised property of *O*, take the present interest in fee simple subject to executory limitation that was retained by *O*. There are no grandchildren at the time the devise becomes effective (*O*'s death) when the interest of the grandchildren is ready for distribution. Therefore, the class of grandchildren will close only on the death of all of *O*'s children, the grandchildren's parents (natural closing). The rule of convenience does not apply.

58.   *I.   None.* The grandchildren who are alive and entitled to distribution at the time of the devise close the class at that time and take a fee simple absolute without having to share it with later-born grandchildren.

59.   *D.   Contingent remainder* in fee simple absolute shared with the unborn children of *A*. There is a condition precedent of survival before *B*'s interest or the interest of any child of *A* vests.

60.   *C.   Reversion* in fee simple absolute. If *B* or any child survives *A*, the reversion does not take; it is divested. If no children survive *A*, the reversion becomes a present interest in *O*.

61.   *H.   Fee tail.* "Her issue" are words of limitation that mean the same as "heirs of her body."

62.   *D.   Contingent remainder* in fee simple absolute. The word "or" is usually construed as disjunctive, giving alternative contingent remainders to *B* and to her children. The condition precedent to *B*'s interest is survivorship of *A*'s fee tail; the condition precedent to the children's interest is the failure of *B* to survive *A*'s fee tail. If *B* dies before the termination of *A*'s fee tail, the class of *B*'s children closes naturally to include all *B*'s children who were alive (including conceived, if later born alive) between the time of the conveyance and the time of *B*'s death. The children who are alive, and the holders of the interests of those children who were members but died, take a vested remainder in fee simple absolute (unless there is a child in gestation at the time of *B*'s death, in which case they take a vested remainder subject to open in a fee simple subject to executory limitation).

63.   *H.   Fee tail. A* has a present interest in a life estate, *B* has a contingent remainder in fee tail.

64.   *O.   Fee simple subject to executory limitation. X* and *Y* have a vested remainder subject to open in fee simple subject to executory limitation, and *C*'s unborn children have an executory interest in fee simple absolute. The class of *C*'s children will close when *C* dies or when *X* and *Y* are entitled to distribution, whichever is sooner.

65. *B.   Executory interest* in a life estate pur autre vie (for the life of *S*). *O* has a present interest in fee simple subject to executory limitation, with the estate subject to the condition of a child of *A* reaching age twelve. *X*'s life estate pur autre vie is shared with *A*'s unborn children. When *X* reaches twelve, he will be entitled to distribution. His executory interest will transform into a present interest subject to open, and *O*'s reversion will be divested. The class will close and will include all children born (or in gestation if later born alive). The children under twelve continue to hold an executory interest. As each child reaches age twelve, he or she takes a share in *X*'s present interest subject to open. When there are no more members under twelve, the present interest is no longer subject to open. The life estate pur autre vie held by the children will end when *S* dies.

66. *B.   Executory interest* in fee simple absolute following the life estate pur autre vie in *A*'s children. When *X*'s executory interest transforms into a present interest, *B*'s executory interest transforms into a vested remainder following *X*'s life estate pur autre vie. The death of *S* terminates the children's estate, and *B*'s vested remainder becomes a present interest.

67. *J.   None of the above is correct. X* has a vested remainder subject to open plus an executory interest. As for *X*'s vested remainder subject to open, *X*'s estate in this interest is a fee simple subject to executory limitation because it is subject to being partially cut short each time a member of the class of children reaches 21 and takes a share in *X*'s estate. Before the children reach 21, they have an executory interest in fee simple absolute. As for *X*'s executory interest, *X*'s estate in this interest is a fee simple absolute shared with the other children. If *A* becomes bankrupt, the executory interest cuts short *A*'s life estate (as well as divesting *X*'s vested remainder).

68. *G.   Life estate subject to executory limitation* subject to being cut short by the condition subsequent of *A*'s bankruptcy. *A*'s children (including *X*) have an executory interest. If bankruptcy occurs and *A* has other children under 21, then the executory interest in *X* will cut short *A*'s life estate to become a present interest subject to open in a fee simple subject to executory limitation. The class will close and *A*'s children who are born will retain an executory interest. If bankruptcy occurs and *A* has not conceived any other children, then the executory interest in *X* will cut short *A*'s life estate to become a present interest in fee simple absolute. The class will close to exclude any other children later born to *A*.

69. *H.   Vested remainder subject to open* in fee simple subject to executory limitation. *A* has a present interest in a life estate. The class has not closed yet, because *A* has not died, nor have *O*'s children. Therefore, *O*'s unborn grandchildren have an executory interest that stands ready to partially cut short *X*'s estate whenever a grandchild is born.

70. *B.   Executory interest* in fee simple absolute. See problem 69 above.

71. *B.   Executory interest* in fee simple absolute. Upon *A*'s death *X* is entitled to distribution of his share, and the rule of convenience closes the class of grandchildren. *Y* is conceived and will be born alive later. Therefore, *Y* is a member of the class. Since *Y* has not yet been born, her interest is still contingent on birth. Therefore, *Y* has an executory interest that stands ready to partially cut short *X*'s interest upon her birth.

72. *I.   None.* The class closes to exclude any future-conceived grandchildren.

73. *I.   None.* When *X* dies, his vested remainder subject to open descends to *M* as his only heir through intestate succession. When *A* dies *M* is entitled to distribution of her share, and the rule of convenience closes the class of grandchildren to exclude any future-conceived grandchildren. Note that *M* is the one who has received the interest of a member of the class under the rule of convenience.

74. *B.   Executory interest* in fee simple absolute. There are no grandchildren one year after *A*'s death when the interest of the grandchildren is ready for distribution. Therefore, the class of grandchildren will close only on the death of all of *O*'s children, the grandchildren's parents (natural closing). The rule of convenience does not apply.

75. *B.   Executory interest* in fee simple absolute. There are no children of *B* who have reached 15 one year after *A*'s death. *X* is 13 years old. Since the time designated in the conveyance for distribution is the later of two events (passage of one year from the termination of *A*'s life estate and the attainment of 15 by one of *B*'s children), the class does not close.

76. *A.   Present interest* in fee simple subject to executory limitation. At the time of the conveyance, *O* retained a reversion following *A*'s life estate. When *A* died, the reversion transformed into a present interest. At that time, *O*'s fee simple subject to executory limitation was subject to two conditions subsequent, that is, the passage of one year and the attainment of 15 by a child of *B*. One year after *A*'s death, *O*'s fee simple subject to executory limitation is subject to one condition subsequent, the attainment of 15 by a child of *B*.

77. *I.   None.* *X* is 16. When he reached 15, the time designated in the conveyance for distribution occurred and the class closed. *X* took a present interest in fee simple absolute which he now holds. *O*'s present interest in a fee simple subject to executory limitation was divested by the occurrence of the condition subsequent. The future-born children of *B* are not entitled to become members of the class.

78. *I.   None.* The time for distribution, the termination of *A*'s fee tail, has arrived. The heirs of *B*'s deceased child hold that child's interest. Therefore, the class closes and the future-born children of *B* are not entitled to become members of the class.

79. *I.   None.* The heirs of *B*'s deceased child take that child's inter-
     est, which at the time of the child's death was a vested remain-
     der subject to open. Upon the termination of *A*'s fee tail, this
     remainder becomes a present interest in fee simple absolute.

80. *L.   Fee simple absolute* shared with *X*. The time for distribution
     is one year after the termination of *A*'s fee tail. Since there are no
     members of the class of *B*'s children in existence at that time, the
     rule of convenience does not apply. The class remains open
     until it closes naturally. When *X* and *Y* are born, they take a pres-
     ent interest subject to open in a fee simple subject to executory
     limitation (the condition subsequent that would partially cut
     short their interest is the birth of other children to *B*). When *B*
     dies, the class closes naturally, and the estate held by *X* and *Y*
     becomes a fee simple absolute.

81. *A.   Present interest* subject to open in a fee simple subject to ex-
     ecutory limitation. The time for distribution (*Y*'s reaching 21) is
     immediate. The class is closed at the time of the conveyance,
     and the only members are *X* and *Y*. *X* has an executory interest
     until she reaches 21.

82. *I.   None.* The class is closed.

83. *A.   Present interest* subject to open in a fee simple subject to ex-
     ecutory limitation. The time for distribution (*A*'s death and *Y*'s
     reaching 21) occurs at *A*'s death. The class closes at that time,
     and the only members are *X*, *Y*, and *Z* (who is in gestation at the
     time of *A*'s death). At *A*'s death *X* and *Z* have an executory in-
     terest until each should reach 21. Two years after *A*'s death when
     X dies, *X*'s interest is destroyed (it does not pass to heirs) for
     failure of *X* to satisfy the condition precedent of reaching age 21.

84. *B.   Executory interest* in a fee simple absolute. *Z* continues to
     hold this interest two years after *A*'s death. If *Z* reaches 21, *Z*
     will share a present interest in fee simple absolute with *Y*.

85. *A.   Present interest* subject to open shared with *Y* in a fee simple
     subject to executory limitation. The time for distribution to the
     class is immediately upon conveyance. Since there are no class
     members to take at that time, the rule of convenience does not
     apply. The class will remain open until it closes naturally upon
     B's death.

86. *A.   Present interest* subject to open in a fee simple subject to ex-
     ecutory limitation. Although a child in gestation ordinarily
     must be born before she will receive a vested interest, the law
     creates a fiction in this case to give *X* a vested interest at the
     point of *A*'s death in order to avoid a reversion in *O*. Immedi-
     ately before *A*'s death, *X* held an executory interest that stood
     ready to cut short *O*'s reversion upon *X*'s birth in order to
     become a vested remainder subject to open. This process was
     accelerated by *A*'s death. Although *X* takes a vested present in-
     terest at *A*'s death, *X*'s entitlement to distribution of this vested
     interest most likely will be postponed until *X* is born. Therefore,
     until *X* is entitled to distribution by her birth, the time for distri-

bution has not arrived and the class will remain open to receive any other children conceived before *X*'s birth (as long as they are later born alive).

87. *L. Fee simple absolute.* At the time of the conveyance, *A* has a present interest in a life estate; *B* has a vested remainder in a fee tail; *C* has a vested remainder in a life estate; *X* has a vested remainder subject to open in a fee simple subject to executory limitation; and *D*'s unborn children have an executory interest in a fee simple absolute. When *X* dies, *M* takes his interest. The plane crash causes *A, B,* and *C* to lose their interests, and *M*'s vested remainder subject to open transforms into a present interest subject to open. At this time the class of *D*'s children closes to include only *M* and the child in gestation. The child in gestation has an executory interest in a fee simple absolute. Two weeks later when the child in gestation dies before birth, *M*'s estate becomes a fee simple absolute.

88. *I. None.* The class closes when *M* becomes entitled to distribution at the time of the plane crash.

89. *B. Executory interest* in a fee simple absolute. The time for distribution in this conveyance is the time of the conveyance. Since there were no children in existence at that time, the rule of convenience does not apply. The class will close only upon *A*'s death. Even though it is medically impossible for *A* to have any more children at the age of 110, the law creates the fiction that she can bear children until she dies. Therefore, *X* has a present interest subject to open in a fee simple subject to executory limitation, and the unborn children have the executory interest that stands ready to partially cut short *X*'s estate upon their birth.

90. *D. Contingent remainder in fee simple absolute* shared with *X, Z,* and the unborn grandchildren. This contingent remainder follows *A*'s present interest in fee tail and accompanies *O*'s reversion in fee simple absolute.

91. *B. Executory interest* in a fee simple absolute. At the time of *A*'s death, *Y* is the only grandchild who has reached age ten. *Y*'s contingent remainder transforms into a present interest subject to open in a fee simple subject to executory limitation. The class closes, and *X* and *G* who are the only remaining members of the class hold an executory interest that stands ready to partially cut short *Y*'s estate whenever each reaches age ten.

92. *I. None. H* never receives any interest or estate because he is conceived after the class closes.

93. *I. None.* Although there are no members of the class alive at *H*'s birth, *Y*'s present interest is held by *Y*'s heirs. *Y*'s heirs took a present interest subject to open in a fee simple subject to executory limitation when *Y* died. When *G* and *X* died before either had turned ten, *G* and *X* lost their interest and *Y*'s heirs then had a present interest in a fee simple absolute.

94. *P. None.* The class closes immediately upon conveyance and the only member of the class is *X. Y* and *Z* take no interest.

When X dies, the only survivor dies and the life estate held by X is terminated. O's reversion that has been inherited by O's heirs becomes a present interest in fee simple absolute.

95. *O.   Fee simple subject to executory limitation.* The time for distribution to the class of O's grandchildren is the time of conveyance. Since there are no members of the class at that time (R is not born alive), the rule of convenience does not apply. The class can only close naturally by the death of all O's children, the parents of O's grandchildren. At the time of T's birth, both S and T share a present interest subject to open in a fee simple subject to executory limitation. The unborn grandchildren have an executory interest.

96. *A.   Present interest in a fee simple absolute.* When A dies, her present interest in fee tail is inherited by her two children. The fee tail terminates upon their deaths which occur eleven years after the conveyance. One year after the termination of the fee tail, S takes a present interest subject to open in a fee simple subject to executory limitation. The class has already closed naturally by this point because B has died and no more children of B can be born; however, T's interest is still contingent on his getting married. When T marries three years later, T's executory interest transforms into S's present interest and they both share a present interest in fee simple absolute.

97. *L.   Fee simple absolute.* See problem 96 above.

98. *I.   None.* The interest in A's children is terminated by the occurrence of the condition subsequent, X going to law school. Z never takes any interest.

99. *A.   Present interest* subject to open in a fee simple subject to executory limitation. When X goes to law school, the time for distribution to B's children has arrived. Since there are no children in existence, the rule of convenience does not apply. The class will close only naturally when B dies. When X goes to law school, O takes a present interest in fee simple subject to executory limitation. This present interest is divested when F is born. Upon F's birth F takes a present interest subject to open in a fee simple subject to executory limitation. This interest remains subject to open when G is born because B is still alive.

100. *A.   Present interest* subject to open in a fee simple subject to executory limitation. G takes a share in F's interest because the class has not yet closed.

Rules for Identification of the Conveyance

Over the years a number of rules have developed to determine the meaning of certain types of conveyances. These rules have been gathered and summarized in the ten rules below.

A. NO GAP IN SEISIN

If there is a gap in the conveyance, it must be filled with a reversionary interest.

> *Example*: Where *O* conveys "to *A* for life," *A*'s life estate is followed by a reversion.
> *Example*: Where *O* conveys "to *A* in fee simple determinable," *A*'s estate is followed by a possibility of reverter.
> *Example*: Where *O* conveys "to *A* in fee tail and then one day later to *B* in fee simple absolute," *A*'s estate is followed by a reversion in *O* which lasts for one day. Technically, *O* has retained a reversion in fee simple (*O*'s original estate) that is limited by a condition subsequent (the passage of one day after the termination of *A*'s fee tail). *B* has an executory interest that springs from *O*'s estate when *O*'s estate is cut short by the condition subsequent. Therefore, *O* has a reversion in fee simple subject to executory limitation.

B. PIGGYBACK RULE

A nonfreehold interest followed by a freehold interest is in fact concurrent with the freehold interest if the freehold interest is in a born, ascertained person and not a future interest subject to a condition precedent.

Some texts describe the freehold interest that "follows" a nonfreehold interest as a remainder or a reversion. This may be a *modern usage*, but it is both confusing and misleading. Not only is it confusing when applying the rules of estates and future interests, but the concept of an interest subject to a term is not so unusual that it need be avoided. The landlord-tenant relationship evokes the idea of an owner holding his interest concurrently with a tenant in possession.

> *Example*: Where O conveys "to A for ten years and then to B in fee simple absolute," B has a present interest in fee simple absolute subject to a term of years in A, that is, B is the landlord and A is the tenant.
>
> *Example*: Where O conveys "to A for ten years and then to B if B gets married," O has a present interest in a freehold (fee simple subject to executory limitation) subject to a term of years in A, and B has an executory interest in fee simple absolute. (Note that "subject to" is used in two different senses here.) When the condition precedent ("if B gets married") is satisfied, the executory interest becomes a present interest in fee simple absolute either subject to the term in A or not, depending on whether A's term has expired.
>
> *Example*: Where O conveys "to A for life, then to B for ten years, then to C if C gets married," A has a present interest in a life estate, C has a contingent remainder in fee simple, O has a reversion in fee simple subject to a term of years in B. If C gets married, C's contingent remainder vests in interest and O's reversion is divested. B's term of years then rests on C's estate.

C. "DIE WITHOUT ISSUE" CONSTRUCTION

Issue refers to the line of descendants of one's body. "Die without issue" may mean three different things: (1) dying without having issue at the point of one's death; (2) dying without ever having had issue; or (3) dying without having issue at the point of one's death or, if issue do exist, termination of the line of issue. The first meaning is a "definite failure of issue" construction. It refers to failure of issue at a definite point in time: someone's death. The second is not usually used. The third is an "indefinite failure of issue" construction. It refers to failure of issue at an indefinite point in time: whenever there are no issue from the point of death onwards. The preference today is for the definite failure of issue construction except where an indefinite failure of issue construction may be used to complement a fee tail.

> *Example*: Where O conveys "to A and her heirs, but if A dies without issue, to B and his heirs," A has a present interest in fee simple subject to executory limitation and B has an executory interest in fee simple absolute. The preferred definite failure of issue construction is used. B's interest will become a present interest if A has no issue at her death. If A has issue alive at her death, B's interest is destroyed.

Example: Where *O* conveys "to *A* and her issue, but if *A* dies without issue, then to *B* and his heirs," *A* has a fee tail and *B* has a vested remainder in fee simple absolute. The indefinite failure of issue construction is used. "Issue" means the whole line of descendants of one's body, and in this context "and her issue" are words of limitation giving *A* a fee tail. The condition "if *A* dies without issue" is taken to mean "whenever the line of *A*'s issue runs out from the point of *A*'s death." In this sense the condition is superfluous because it merely restates the nature of *A*'s fee tail. Whenever the fee tail terminates the next interest will take. Since the condition is superfluous, it is not treated as a condition precedent to *B*'s interest, and the remainder in *B* is vested.

D. SUBSUMPTION RULE

A condition that merely states the essence of an estate in a conveyance is not a condition in that conveyance.

Example: Where *O* conveys "to *A* for life, but if *A* dies, then to *B* in fee simple absolute," *B* has a vested remainder because *A*'s death terminates *A*'s life estate by definition of that estate. Mention of *A*'s death in the condition is considered superfluous and therefore the condition is ignored. Technically, *A*'s life estate might terminate unnaturally by forfeiture before *A*'s death, but this possibility is not considered when rendering the condition ineffective.

Example: Where *O* conveys "to *A* and his heirs, but if *A* dies, then to *B* in fee simple absolute," *A* has a life estate and *B* a vested remainder, because the condition becomes part of the words of limitation to define *A*'s life estate.

Example: Where *O* conveys "to *A* for life, then if *A* dies before *B*, to *B* for life," *A* has a life estate and *B* a vested remainder for life, leaving a reversion in *O*. The condition is considered superfluous.

Example: Where *O* conveys "to *A* for life, then if *A* dies before *B*, to *B* in fee simple absolute," *A* has a life estate and *B* a contingent remainder in fee simple absolute. The condition is *not* superfluous. If *B* dies before *A*, *B*'s interest is destroyed because of the condition; without the condition *B*'s interest would be vested from the time of the conveyance and would pass to *B*'s heirs upon *B*'s death before *A* (if *B* has not conveyed or devised it).

E. MODIFIED RULE IN WILD'S CASE

A conveyance "to *A* and *A*'s children" generally gives a fee simple estate to *A* and *A*'s children as a tenancy in common if the children are alive at the time of the conveyance. There is some difference of opinion on how *A* and her children take. If they take as a class, they share equally. If they take an individual gift and a class gift, it may be an undivided one-half gift to *A* and an undivided one-half gift to the children. If the children are not yet alive at the time of the conveyance, the conveyance "to *A* and *A*'s children" generally gives a life estate to *A* followed by a contingent remainder in the unborn children. (The first resolution in Wild's Case (1599) is to interpret the devise "to *A* and his children" (children not living) as a fee tail in *A*; the second resolution in Wild's Case is to interpret the devise "to *A* and his children" (children then living) as a life estate held concurrently by *A* and his children as joint tenants. Neither of these resolutions is the preferred view any longer.)

If the conveyance "to *A* and *A*'s children" is postponed to some future date, such as in a conveyance "to *X* for life, then to *A* and *A*'s children," this modified Rule in Wild's Case still applies. The time for determining whether children have been born so as to share a tenancy in common with *A* is generally held to be the time that the postponed gift takes effect, such as in this example when *X* dies. Note also that this Rule is a rule of construction that will give way to a contrary intent expressed by the grantor.

F. PREFERENCE FOR VESTING EXCEPTION

Conditions are determined to be precedent or subsequent in large part by the way they read. Professor George Haskins, my teacher and mentor, had a general rule that if a condition describes the terms on which *X takes* the interest it is precedent; if it describes the terms on which he *loses* it, it is subsequent.

> *Example*: Where *O* conveys "to *A* for life, then to *B* and her heirs, but if *B* gets married, then to *C* and his heirs," the but-if condition describes the terms on which *B* loses her interest and *C* takes his. *B* has a vested remainder in fee simple subject to executory limitation and *C* has an executory interest in fee simple.
>
> *Example*: On the other hand, where *O* conveys "to *A* for life, then if *B* gets married, to *B* and her heirs, otherwise to *C* and his heirs," *B* and *C* both have contingent remainders.

One exception to this rule of construction is worth noting. Due to a preference for vesting, two future interests, each with an apparent condition precedent, may not be classified as contingent remainders but rather as a vested remainder subject to divestment followed by an executory interest when the two conditions refer to an age contingency and appear together. This preference for vesting exception exists to avoid the destruction of contingent remainders through the Merger Rule and the Destructibility of Contingent Remainders Rule (both discussed below).

Example: Where *O* conveys "to *A* for life, then to *B* if *B* reaches 21, but if *B* does not reach 21, then to *C*," the two conditions may be read together as one condition that is subsequent to *B*'s estate and precedent to *C*'s interest. *B* has a vested remainder subject to divestment (more particularly, a vested remainder in fee simple subject to executory limitation) and *C* has an executory interest in fee simple absolute. If the conditions were separated in this conveyance, *B* and *C* would have alternative contingent remainders. Examples of conveyances with alternative contingent remainders are where *O* conveys "to *A* for life, then if *B* reaches 21 to *B*, but if *B* does not reach 21, then to *C*"; where *O* conveys "to *A* for life, then to *B* if *B* reaches 21, then to *C* if *B* does not reach 21"; and where *O* conveys "to *A* for life, then if *B* reaches 21, to *B*, then to *C* if *B* does not reach 21."

G. BACKUP RULE

A contingent remainder is always accompanied by a vested remainder or a reversion.

Example: Where *O* conveys "to *A* for life, then to *B* if *B* gets married," *B* has a contingent remainder and *O* has a reversion.

Example: Where *O* conveys "to *A* for life, then to *B* for life if *B* gets married, then to *C*," *C* has a vested remainder accompanying *B*'s contingent remainder.

Example: Where *O* conveys "to *A* for life, then if *B* gets married, to *B*, then to *C*," *B* and *C* have alternative contingent remainders, each in fee simple absolute, and both of which are accompanied by a reversion in *O*. Note that *C* cannot have a vested remainder in fee simple absolute because the vesting of *B*'s contingent remainder would divest *C*'s vested remainder (not merely postpone it) and such divestment is not permitted. *O*'s reversion is the only type of interest that can be divested in such a case.

Example: Where *O* conveys "to *A* for life, then to such of *B*'s children who reach 21, then to *C*," the condition precedent is incorporated in the words of purchase "to *B*'s children," and *B* and *C* have alternative contingent remainders for the same reason given in the example above.

H. MERGER RULE

Merger occurs when one person holds two immediately successive vested interests (or contingent interests that are contingent on the satisfaction of the same condition precedent) or two vested interests that are successive except for intervening contingent remainder(s). There are two exceptions to the rule: (1) *A fee tail does not merge with a fee simple*, and (2) *two vested interests simultaneously created in the same person do not merge in that person if there is an intervening contingent remainder created in another person at the same time.*

Although absent from the literature, perhaps a third exception should be added to the rule as well: (3) *A life estate pur autre vie does not merge with a fee tail, and a life estate does not merge with a fee tail owned by one other than the original owner.* Since a life estate pur autre vie has the capacity to outlast a fee tail, and a fee tail has aspects that are absent from the life estate pur autre vie, the merger of the two cannot produce an estate that incorporates the full extent of both. The same can be said for the life estate and the fee tail owned by one other than the original owner. There is no such estate as a fee tail pur autre vie. Therefore, merger should be disallowed.

> *Example*: Where *O* conveys "to *A* for life, then to *B* if *B* gets married," *B* has a contingent remainder and *O* has a reversion. If *A* conveys his interest back to *O* (or *O* conveys her reversion to *A*), the intervening contingent remainder in *B* is destroyed. The present interest in a life estate pur autre vie in *O* and the reversion in fee simple absolute in *O* (or the present interest in a life estate in *A* and the reversion in fee simple absolute in *A*) merge to form one present interest in fee simple absolute.
>
> *Example*: Where *O* conveys "to *A* in fee tail, then to *B* if *B* gets married," *B* has a contingent remainder and *O* has a reversion. If *A* conveys to *O* (or *O* to *A*), the contingent remainder is not destroyed because a fee simple does not merge with a fee tail under the first exception to the merger rule.
>
> *Example*: Where *O* conveys "to *A* for life, then if *B* gets married, to *B* for life, then to *C* in fee tail," *A* has a present interest in a life estate, *B* has a contingent remainder, *C* has a vested remainder in fee tail, and *O* has a reversion. If *A* conveys to *C* (or *C* to *A*), the contingent remainder should not be destroyed according to the suggested third exception to the merger rule.
>
> *Example*: Where *O* conveys "to *A* for life, then to *B* for life if *B* gets married, then to *A* in fee simple absolute," *B* has a contingent remainder and *A* has a life estate plus a vested remainder in fee simple absolute. *B*'s contingent remainder is not destroyed because of the second exception to the merger rule. But if *A* conveys away both his interests and they come into the hands of one person, *B*'s contingent remainder is merged out. Thus, if *A* conveys both his interests to *X*, *X* receives a present interest in a life estate pur autre vie and a vested remainder in fee simple absolute, which merge to form one present interest in fee simple absolute.
>
> *Example*: Where *O* conveys "to *A* for life, then if *B* gets married, to *B* for life and then to *C*, and if *B* does not get married, to *D* for life and then to *E*," *B*, *C*, *D*, and *E* have contingent remainders. *B* (followed by *C*) is prepared to take a vested interest if *B* gets married before the

death of *A*. *D* (followed by *E*) is prepared to take a vested interest if *B* does not get married before the death of *A*. In the meantime, *O*'s reversion is the only vested interest following *A*'s present interest in a life estate. If *E* conveys her interest to *D*, *D*'s contingent remainder in a life estate merges with the contingent remainder in fee simple absolute received from *E* and forms a contingent remainder in fee simple absolute.

Note that the Merger Rule is not only a rule for identification but also a rule to govern events subsequent to the conveyance.

I. RULE IN SHELLEY'S CASE

If a conveyance or will gives a freehold estate in real property to a person and a remainder to that same person's heirs (or heirs of the body), and the estates are both legal or both equitable, the remainder is considered a remainder in fee simple (or fee tail) in the ancestor. This rule applies even where the freehold estate is held by the ancestor as a cotenant, and where the freehold estate is held as a vested remainder preceding the remainder in the heirs or as a contingent remainder subject to the same condition precedent as the following remainder in the heirs. The Rule in Shelley's Case (1581) operates on a delayed basis when the requirements of the Rule are satisfied at a later time, such as when the interest in the ancestor is subject to a condition precedent not made applicable to the remainder interest in the heirs and the condition precedent is satisfied, or the interest in the heirs is an executory interest that later becomes a remainder. Furthermore, the Rule in Shelley's Case is a rule of law, not a rule of construction.

> *Example*: Where *O* conveys "to *A* for life, then to *B* for life, then to *A*'s heirs," *A* has a present interest in a life estate plus a vested remainder in fee simple absolute that follows a vested remainder in a life estate in *B*. (There is no merger because *B* has an intervening vested remainder.)
>
> *Example*: Where *O* conveys "to *A* for life, then to *A*'s heirs," *A* has a present interest in a life estate and, under the Rule in Shelley's Case, a vested remainder in fee simple absolute. Under the Merger Rule, these two interests merge to form a present interest in fee simple absolute.
>
> *Example*: Where *O* conveys "to *A* for life, then to *A*'s heirs if *B* gets married," *A* has a present interest in a life estate plus a contingent remainder in fee simple absolute (subject to the condition precedent that *B* get married). *O* has a reversion in fee simple absolute.

Note that many states have abrogated the Rule in Shelley's Case.

J.   DOCTRINE OF WORTHIER TITLE

The attempt of a grantor to create a future interest (remainder or executory interest) in real or personal property in his heirs (not heirs of the body) creates instead a reversionary interest in the grantor. This is a rule of construction, which means that the presumption created by the rule can be rebutted by the manifestation of a contrary intent. There are two branches of the Doctrine of Worthier Title. The testamentary branch is largely moribund and is omitted from discussion in this book. The inter vivos branch described here continues to play an important role in modern law.

> *Example*: Where O conveys "to A for life, then to the heirs of O," A has a present interest in a life estate and O has a reversion.
> *Example*: Where O conveys "to A and her heirs until (or but if) A gets married, then to the heirs of O," A has a present interest in a fee simple determinable and O has a possibility of reverter.

Note that some states have abrogated the Doctrine of Worthier Title.

Problem Set III

The problems in this section ask for a description of an interest or an estate. The answers for interest are:

    A.   present interest
    B.   executory interest
    C.   reversion
    D.   contingent remainder
    E.   right of reentry
    F.   vested remainder
    G.   possibility of reverter
    H.   vested remainder subject to open
    I.   none
    J.   none of the above is correct

The answers for estate are:

    A.   term of years
    B.   term of years determinable
    C.   life estate
    D.   life estate pur autre vie
    E.   life estate determinable
    F.   life estate subject to condition subsequent
    G.   life estate subject to executory limitation
    H.   fee tail
    I.   fee tail determinable

    J.   fee tail subject to condition subsequent
    K. fee tail subject to executory limitation
    L.   fee simple absolute
    M. fee simple determinable
    N. fee simple subject to condition subsequent
    O. fee simple subject to executory limitation
    P.   none
    Q. none of the above is correct

Problems

O conveys to Max for two years, then to Carl for life, then to the heirs of his boss Fred and their heirs.

    101.   What is Max's estate?
    102.   What is Carl's interest?
    103.   What is Fred's heirs' interest?
    104.   What is *O*'s interest?

O conveys to Pam for life, then to Bill and his heirs, but if Bill dies without issue, then to Cathy and her heirs.

    105.   What is Bill's interest?
    106.   What is *O*'s interest?

O conveys to Andy and his children. Andy has a son, Casper, and a grandson, Jim.

    107.   What is Andy's estate?

O conveys to *A* for ten years and then to *A*'s heirs.

    108.   What is the interest of *A*'s heirs?

O conveys to *A* and his heirs, but if *A* dies, to *B* and his heirs.

    109.   What is *A*'s estate?

O conveys to *A* and his heirs to take effect after *A* gets married.

    110.   What is *A*'s interest?

O conveys to Andy and his children. Andy has no children at the time.

    111.   What is Andy's estate?

O conveys to *A* for life, then if *B* has a son to *B* and his heirs, but if *B* does not have a son to *C* and his heirs.

    112.   What is *C*'s interest?

O conveys to *A* and his heirs until 20 years after *A*'s death, then to *B* and his heirs.

113.   What is *B*'s interest?

O conveys to *A* and his heirs until *A* gets married, then to the heirs of *O*.

114.   What is the interest in *O*'s heirs?

O conveys to *A* for 30 years, then to *B* and his heirs if *B* gets married.

115.   What is *O*'s estate?

O conveys to *A* for life, then to *B* for one day, then to the heirs of *A*.

116.   What is the interest in *A*'s heirs?

O conveys to *A* for life, then one day after *A*'s death to *O*'s heirs.

117.   What is the interest in *O*'s heirs?

O conveys to *A* for life, then to *B* and her heirs if *B* reaches 15, but if she dies before reaching 15, to the heirs of *B*.

118.   What is the interest in the heirs of *B*?

O conveys to *A* for life, then to *B* for life if *B* has a son, then to the heirs of *A* and their heirs.

119.   What is *A*'s interest?

O conveys to *A* and the heirs of his body, then to *B* for life if *B* gets married.

120.   What is *O*'s interest?

O conveys to *A* for life, then to such of *A*'s children as shall attain the age of 21 and their heirs, then to *C* and his heirs. At the time of the conveyance, *B* is *A*'s only child and is 19 years old.

121.   What is *B*'s interest?
122.   What is *O*'s interest?

O devises to *A* for life, then to *B* if *B* has children. At *O*'s death, *B* has no children and *A* is *O*'s only heir.

123.   What is *B*'s interest?

O conveys to *A* for life, then to *O*'s son *B* and his heirs. If *O* were to die at this point, she would have no other heirs in the world but *B*.

124.   What is *B*'s interest?

O conveys to *A* for life, then to *O*'s children who reach 21 and their heirs. *O* has two children who are ages five and ten.

125.   What is *O*'s children's interest?

O conveys to *A* for life or until she gets married, then to the heirs of *A*.

126. What is *A*'s interest?

O devises to *A* and his issue, but if *A* dies without issue, then to *B* and her heirs.

127. What is the estate in *A*'s issue?
128. What is *B*'s interest?
129. What is *O*'s interest?

O conveys to *A*, but if *A* gets married, then to the heirs of *A*.

130. What is *A*'s heirs' interest?
131. What is *A*'s estate?

O conveys to *A* and the heirs of his body, then to *B* for life if *B* has a son, then to *C* for life.

132. What is *C*'s interest?

O conveys to *A* for life, then to *B*, but if *B* gets married, then to *C*.

133. What is *C*'s interest?

O conveys to *A* and her heirs as long as *A* has no son, otherwise to the heirs of *O*.

134. What is *O*'s heirs' interest?
135. What is *O*'s interest?

O conveys to *A* for life or until he has a grandson, then to the heirs of *B*.

136. What is *B*'s heirs' interest?

O conveys to *A* for life, then to the issue of *A*. *A* has issue at the time of the conveyance.

137. What is *A*'s estate?
138. What is *O*'s interest?

O conveys to *A* for life, then to *B* if *A* dies before *B*.

139. What is *B*'s interest?

O conveys to *A* for life, then to *B* for life, then to the heirs of *A* if *A* gets married.

140. What is *A*'s interest?

O conveys to *A* for life, then to *B* and her heirs if *A* dies without a son, but if he dies with a son, to the heirs of *A*.

141. What is the interest in the heirs of *A*?

O conveys to *A* for life, then to *A*'s heirs for the life of the survivor.

142. What is *A*'s estate?

O conveys to *A* for life, and if she gets married, then, upon the termination of her life estate, to the heirs of *A*.

    143.   What is *A*'s estate?

O conveys to *A* and her issue, but if *B* gets married, then to the heirs of *A*.

    144.   What is *A*'s estate?

O conveys to *A* for life, then, if *B* gets married, to *B* for life unless *B* divorces, otherwise to *C* and her heirs.

    145.   What is *B*'s estate?
    146.   What is *C*'s interest?

O conveys to *A* and *B* for their joint lives, then to the heirs of *A*.

    147.   What is *A*'s interest?

O conveys to *A* for life, then, if *A* dies without a son, to *B* and his heirs, but if *A* dies with a son, to the heirs of *B*.

    148.   What is the interest of *B*'s heirs?

O conveys to *A* for life, then to *B* and his heirs as long as *B* does not get married, then to *O*'s heirs.

    149.   What is *B*'s estate?

O conveys to *A* for life, then to *B* for life if *A* dies before *B*.

    150.   What is *B*'s interest?

O conveys to *A* during widowhood, then to *B*. At the time of the conveyance, *A* is a widow.

    151.   What is *A*'s estate?
    152.   What is *B*'s interest?

O conveys to *A* for life, then to *B*'s oldest daughter. *B*'s oldest daughter happens to be *S*.

    153.   What is *S*'s interest?

O conveys to *A* for life, then to her surviving children, then to *B*.

    154.   What is *B*'s interest?

O conveys to *A* and his heirs, but if *A* dies without issue, then to *B* and his heirs as long as *B* is alive.

    155.   What is *B*'s estate?

O conveys to *A* for life, then, if *B* gets married, to *B* for life, then to the heirs of *B*.

156.   What is *B*'s interest?

O conveys to *A* for life, then to *B* and the heirs of his body, but if *B* dies without issue, then to *C* for life, then to *D* and her heirs.

157.   What is *C*'s interest?
158.   What is *D*'s interest?

O conveys to *A* for life, then to *B* for life, then, if *A* dies before *C*, to *C* for life.

159.   What is *C*'s interest?

O conveys to *A* for life, then to the heirs of *O*, with the express desire to leave nothing in the property in himself despite the Doctrine of Worthier Title.

160.   What is the interest of *O*'s heirs?

O conveys to *B* for life, then to *C* and his heirs when *C* reaches 21, but if *C* dies under 21, to *D* and her heirs. *C* is two years old at the time of the conveyance.

161.   What is *C*'s interest?

O conveys to *A* for the life of *B* in trust for *B* for life, then to the heirs of *B*.

162.   What is *B*'s estate?

O devises to *A* and the heirs of her body, then to *B* for life, then to *C* and the heirs of her body, then to *D* as long as *D* remains sober.

163.   What is *C*'s estate?
164.   What is *D*'s estate?
165.   What is the interest of *O*'s heirs?

O conveys to *A* for life, then to *B* if *B* gets married, but if *B* does not get married, then to *C* for life and following *C*'s life estate to *D*.

166.   What is *D*'s interest?
167.   What is *O*'s interest?

O conveys to *A* for life, then to *B*, but if *B* gets married, then to *C* for life and following *C*'s life estate to *D*.

168.   What is *D*'s interest?

O conveys to *A* and the heirs of her body, then to *B* and her children. *B* has no children at the time of the conveyance.

169.   What is *B*'s estate?

O conveys to *A* and the heirs of her body, then to *B* and her children. *B* has one child, *X*, at the time of the conveyance.

170.   What is *B*'s estate?

O conveys to *A* for the life of *B*, then to *A* and the heirs of her body, then to *C* and his heirs.

171.   What is *A*'s estate?

O conveys to *A* for life, then to the heirs of *O*'s body. *O* has no issue at the time of the conveyance.

172.   What is the interest of the heirs of *O*'s body?

O conveys to *A* for life, then to the heirs of *A*'s body. *A* has no issue at the time of the conveyance.

173.   What is the interest of the heirs of *A*'s body?

O conveys to *A* for life or for as long as it takes his sister, *B*, to finish law school in his lifetime, then to *B* for eight years or for as long as it takes *A* to finish law school before the end of that eight years.

174.   What is *A*'s estate?
175.   What is *B*'s estate?

Answers

101.   A.   *Term of years.* It is a fixed calendar time period.
102.   A.   *Present interest* in a life estate under the Piggyback Rule.
103.   D.   *Contingent remainder.* Fred is still alive and his heirs remain unascertained until he dies.
104.   C.   *Reversion* that accompanies the contingent remainder under the Backup Rule.
105.   F.   *Vested remainder* in fee simple subject to executory limitation, followed by an executory interest in fee simple in Cathy. The executory interest in Cathy transforms into a vested remainder (or a present interest if Pam's life estate has terminated) if Bill has no issue at his death. The definite failure of issue construction used here is preferred.
106.   I.   *None.* Orville has no interest left after his conveyance.
107.   L.   *Fee simple absolute* shared with his son Casper as a tenancy in common under the Modified Rule in Wild's Case.
108.   B.   *Executory interest.* The Rule in Shelley's Case does not apply because *A*'s estate is a nonfreehold. *A*'s heirs are not ascertained, so they cannot take a present interest under the Piggyback Rule. *O* retains a present interest in fee simple subject to executory limitation and subject to a term of years in *A*.
109.   C.   *Life estate.* The words of limitation are "and his heirs, but if *A* dies."
110.   B.   *Executory interest* springing from a present interest in fee simple subject to executory limitation retained by *O*.
111.   C.   *Life estate.* The children have a contingent remainder in fee simple under the Modified Rule in Wild's Case.

112. *D. Contingent remainder*. B and C have alternative contingent remainders because each interest is accompanied by a condition that is treated as a condition precedent.

113. *B. Executory interest*. Although a time is specified, it depends on A's death. Therefore, A has a present interest in fee simple subject to executory limitation. B has an executory interest in fee simple absolute.

114. *I. None*. A has a fee simple determinable (note the language of duration in the condition). Under the Doctrine of Worthier Title, O has a possibility of reverter.

115. *O. Fee simple subject to executory limitation* and subject to a term of years in A. B's interest is subject to a condition precedent that prevents it from taking immediately. This same condition is a condition subsequent on O's estate. The term of years rides piggyback on O's freehold estate.

116. *I. None*. The Piggyback Rule makes the freehold interest "following" the term of years a remainder following A's life estate. The Rule in Shelley's Case gives this remainder to A as a vested remainder in fee simple absolute in addition to her present interest in a life estate. The Merger Rule combines the two interests. A has a present interest in fee simple absolute subject to a term of one day in B after A's death.

117. *I. None*. O's heirs do not take an executory interest. Under the Doctrine of Worthier Title, O takes a reversionary interest that merges with his reversion. O's conveyance thus gives A a present interest in a life estate, and O retains a reversion in fee simple absolute.

118. *B. Executory interest*. B has a vested remainder in fee simple subject to executory limitation, given the preference for vesting. B's heirs have an executory interest in fee simple absolute. The condition precedent on the vesting of their executory interest is B's death before age 15, at which point the condition is satisfied and the heirs are ascertained. The Rule in Shelley's Case does not apply where the heirs have an executory interest.

119. *J. None of the above is correct*. A's interests are a present interest in a life estate plus a vested remainder in fee simple absolute. The interest designated for A's heirs is a remainder following A's present interest in a life estate and accompanied by an intervening contingent remainder in a life estate in B. The Rule in Shelley's Case operates to give the remainder designated for A's heirs to A as a vested remainder, leaving the heirs with nothing. The two vested interests in A do not merge out the contingent remainder in B because of an exception to the Merger Rule. (However, A could convey her interests to X, giving X a present interest in fee simple absolute under the Merger Rule and thus destroying B's contingent remainder.)

120. *C. Reversion* to accompany the contingent remainder in B, and, if B's remainder vests, to follow it.

121. *D. Contingent remainder*. Since the condition is incorporated with the words of purchase, A's children have a contingent re-

mainder and *C* has an alternative contingent remainder. Both have estates in fee simple absolute. *A* has a present interest in a life estate, and *O* retains a reversion in fee simple absolute. (*B*'s interest will transform into a vested remainder subject to open in two years if *A*'s life estate has not terminated. This will destroy *C*'s alternative contingent remainder as well as *O*'s reversion.)

122. *C.* *Reversion* which accompanies the alternative contingent remainders until one vests or both are destroyed. If one vests, the reversion is destroyed. If the remainders are destroyed, the reversion takes in their place.

123. *D.* *Contingent remainder.* *O*'s reversion created by *O*'s devise immediately descends to *A* at the same time that *A* receives the present interest in a life estate by *O*'s devise. Since these two vested interests are created simultaneously, they do not merge out the intervening contingent remainder in fee simple absolute in *B*. Therefore, *A* is left with a present interest in a life estate plus a reversion in fee simple absolute.

124. *F.* *Vested remainder* in fee simple. *B* cannot be an heir until *O* dies. The Doctrine of Worthier Title applies to heirs; it does not apply when an heir apparent is designated by name in a conveyance.

125. *D.* *Contingent remainder* in fee simple absolute. *O*'s children are not "heirs," therefore, the Doctrine of Worthier Title does not apply. *O*'s children are a class. The age requirement is a condition precedent to each of the children taking a vested interest. The life estate supports their interest as a remainder. *O* has a reversion to accompany the contingent remainder in *O*'s children under the Backup Rule. (If no child reaches 21 before *A* dies, the interest in *O*'s children is destroyed by the Destructibility of Contingent Remainders Rule. See Chapter 4. If a child reaches 21 before *A* dies, she will receive a vested remainder subject to open (divesting *O*'s reversion), and the other children's contingent remainder will transform into an executory interest. Then upon *A*'s death there will be someone standing ready to take and the class will close. Under the class closing rules, all children alive at that time will be considered part of the class and will take a share in the estate when they reach 21.)

126. *A.* *Present interest.* Before application of the Rule in Shelley's Case, *A* has a life estate determinable, followed by a reversion in *O* (which includes *O*'s possibility of reverter prepared to cut short *A*'s estate upon the happening of the condition subsequent of marriage), and the heirs have a contingent remainder in fee simple absolute. The Rule in Shelley's Case operates to give *A* a vested remainder (which includes the possibility of cutting short *A*'s estate upon the happening of the condition subsequent of marriage) in place of the heirs. Under the Merger Rule, *A*'s present and future interests combine to form a present interest in fee simple absolute. Note that the future

interest that follows the life estate is a remainder even though the life estate may be cut short by a condition subsequent. It takes as a remainder whether the life estate terminates naturally, unnaturally, or by operation of the condition subsequent.

127. *P.   None.* "And his issue" are words of limitation and give no estate to the issue.

128. *F.   Vested remainder* in fee simple. "Die without issue" is given an indefinite failure of issue construction to complement the fee tail in *A*. It thus becomes a superfluous condition that merely states the essence of the fee tail estate and is ignored under the Subsumption Rule.

129. *I.   None.* There is nothing left for *O* to have. This is true whenever a vested remainder in fee simple absolute is created.

130. *B.   Executory interest* in fee simple absolute. The Rule in Shelley's Case does not apply when the future interest in the heirs is an executory interest.

131. *O.   Fee simple subject to executory limitation.* The conditions subsequent that cut short *A*'s estate are *A*'s marriage and the ascertainment of *A*'s heirs (upon *A*'s death). These conditions are also conditions precedent, which must be satisfied before the interest in *A*'s heirs can divest *A*'s present interest and become a present interest.

132. *F.   Vested remainder.* *A* has a present interest in fee tail, *B* has a contingent remainder for life, *C* has a vested remainder for life, and *O* has a reversion.

133. *B.   Executory interest* in fee simple absolute. The preference for vesting gives *B* a vested remainder subject to divestment, or more exactly, a vested remainder in fee simple subject to executory limitation.

134. *I.   None.* The interest is eliminated by the Doctrine of Worthier Title, which gives *O* a possibility of reverter to follow a fee simple determinable in *A*.

135. *G.   Possibility of reverter.* See problem 134 above.

136. *D.   Contingent remainder* in fee simple absolute. *A* has a life estate that may be cut short by a condition subsequent. The contingent remainder in *B*'s heirs is contingent on their being ascertained. *O* has a reversion following the natural termination of *A*'s life estate if not sooner (such as upon the event stated in the condition subsequent). If the heirs are ascertained before *A*'s death and *A*'s having a grandson, they divest *O*'s reversion and take a vested remainder following *A*'s life estate. If *A*'s death or *A*'s having a grandson occurs before the heirs are ascertained, the contingent remainder of the heirs is destroyed by the Destructibility of Contingent Remainders Rule. The Rule in Shelley's Case does not apply because *A* is not the ancestor of *B*'s heirs.

137. *H.   Fee tail.* The Rule in Shelley's Case gives the remainder in the issue (interpreted as heirs of the body) to *A* in fee tail. This remainder merges with *A*'s life estate to give *A* a present interest in fee tail.

138. *C.   Reversion* in fee simple absolute. It follows *A*'s present interest in fee tail.

139. *D.   Contingent remainder* in fee simple absolute. The condition makes a difference whether the remainder in fee simple in *B* will continue after the death of *A* or not. It is not superfluous.

140. *J.   None of the above is correct. A* has a present interest in a life estate plus a contingent remainder in fee simple absolute. The Rule in Shelley's Case operates to give *A* the remainder designated for the heirs of *A*. This remainder is still subject to the condition precedent of marriage. *B*'s vested remainder for life and *O*'s reversion (accompanying *A*'s contingent remainder) remain unaffected.

141. *I.   None. A* has a present interest in a life estate followed by alternative contingent remainders in *B* and, before application of the Rule in Shelley's Case, the heirs of *A*. The preference for vesting exception does not apply here because the contingency does not concern age. The Rule in Shelley's Case applies to give *A* a contingent remainder in fee simple absolute in lieu of *A*'s heirs. *A*'s remainder is contingent on *A*'s dying with a son.

142. *C.   Life estate.* The Rule in Shelley's Case does not operate here since the remainder is in *A*'s heirs for the life of the survivor. It is not simply in *A*'s heirs (that is, in fee simple absolute). *A*'s heirs have a contingent remainder in a life estate pur autre vie, and *O* has a reversion.

143. *Q.   None of the above is correct. A* has a present interest in a life estate. Before application of the Rule in Shelley's Case, the heirs have a contingent remainder in fee simple absolute, and *O* has a reversion. Under the Rule in Shelley's Case, *A* takes the contingent remainder in addition to her present interest in a life estate. There is no merger because the remainder is still contingent upon her marriage.

144. *K.   Fee tail subject to executory limitation.* The heirs have an executory interest in fee simple absolute. *O* has a reversion. The Rule in Shelley's Case does not apply when the heirs have an executory interest.

145. *G.   Life estate subject to executory limitation. B*'s interest is a contingent remainder subject to the condition precedent of marriage. The condition subsequent that stands ready to cut short *B*'s life estate is divorce.

146. *F.   Vested remainder* in fee simple absolute following *A*'s present interest in a life estate. This remainder stands ready to take at any time the preceding estates terminate or are sooner cut short. If *A*'s life estate terminates before *B* gets married, *C*'s interest becomes a present interest in fee simple absolute. If *B* gets married before *A*'s estate terminates, *B*'s interest becomes a vested remainder in a life estate subject to executory limitation. It follows *A*'s life estate and is followed by *C*'s vested remainder, which stands ready to take as soon as *A*'s estate and *B*'s estate terminate (or, in the case of *B*'s estate, if it is sooner cut short by the condition subsequent of divorce).

147. *J. None of the above is correct.* A has a present undivided half interest in a fee simple absolute plus an undivided half interest in a vested remainder in fee simple absolute. Before applying the Rule in Shelley's Case, A and B share as tenants in common in a life estate pur autre vie (life estate measured by the life of the first to die) and the heirs of A have a contingent remainder in fee simple absolute. The Rule applies in the case where there is a cotenancy in the freehold estate. After applying the Rule, A has a vested remainder in place of the interest in her heirs. The Merger Rule causes an undivided half of this remainder to merge with the undivided half interest in the life estate pur autre vie. The other undivided half of A's vested remainder remains to take following B's undivided half interest in the life estate pur autre vie.

148. *D. Contingent remainder* in fee simple absolute. A has a present interest in a life estate. B and B's heirs have alternative contingent remainders in fee simple. The Rule in Shelley's Case does not apply because the interest in the ancestor, B, is subject to a condition precedent different from the condition precedent to the remainder in the heirs.

149. *M. Fee simple determinable.* A has a present interest in a life estate. B has a vested remainder in fee simple determinable. The Doctrine of Worthier Title operates in this case to give a possibility of reverter to O rather than an executory interest to O's heirs.

150. *F. Vested remainder* in a life estate following A's present interest in a life estate and followed by a reversion in O. The condition ("if A dies before B") is considered superfluous under the Subsumption Rule. Although it may be possible for A's life estate to terminate by forfeiture before A's death and later on for B to die before A, a preference for vesting argues for the construction that the condition is superfluous, that is, subsumed in the definition of the preceding life estate, thus giving B a vested remainder that transforms into a present interest whenever A's life estate terminates.

151. *G. Life estate subject to executory limitation.* This seems the logical label to apply. Widowhood is interpreted as a situation that can exist only while a woman remains alive and unmarried. Termination by death makes A's estate a life estate. Since the estate may also be cut short by the condition subsequent of marriage in favor of an interest in the grantee B, it is subject to executory limitation.

152. *F. Vested remainder* in fee simple absolute. B stands ready to take upon the natural termination of A's life estate if not sooner (upon A's marriage). Note that B would have an executory interest if he took only upon A's marriage; however, his vested remainder includes this interest.

153. *F. Vested remainder* in fee simple absolute. S is the oldest daughter at the time of the conveyance. An argument might be made that she has only a contingent remainder if a condition

of survivorship is implied in the conveyance (that is, if *S* must be the oldest daughter of *B living* at the termination of *A*'s life estate in order to take), but a preference for vesting argues against this construction.

154.   D.   *Contingent remainder* in fee simple absolute. The children have a contingent remainder in fee simple absolute dependent on survival. *B* cannot have a vested remainder because the vesting of the children's contingent remainder would divest *B*'s vested remainder (not merely postpone it) and such divestment is not permitted. (See the third example under the Backup Rule.) The nonoccurrence of survival is the condition precedent to *B*'s contingent remainder. *O* has a reversion following *A*'s life estate.

155.   C.   *Life estate. A* has a present interest in fee simple subject to executory limitation. The die-without-issue condition is given a definite failure of issue construction. *B* has an executory interest. *B*'s estate is defined by the words "as long as *B* is alive." Therefore, *B* has a life estate followed by a reversionary interest in *O* in fee simple absolute.

156.   D.   *Contingent remainder* in fee simple absolute. Before application of the Rule in Shelley's Case, *A* has a life estate followed by a reversion in *O*, *B* has a contingent remainder (subject to the condition precedent of marriage) in a life estate followed by a reversion in *O*, and *B*'s heirs have a contingent remainder (marriage condition and heirs unascertained) in fee simple absolute. The Rule in Shelley's Case applies when the freehold is subject to a condition precedent to which the remainder in the heirs also is subject. Here *B*'s contingent remainder and the contingent remainder in the heirs are both subject to the condition precedent of marriage. The Rule in Shelley's Case gives the remainder in *B*'s heirs to *B*. The Merger Rule combines *B*'s two interests.

157.   F.   *Vested remainder* in a life estate. *A* has a present interest in a life estate. *B* has a vested remainder in fee tail. The die-without-issue condition is given an indefinite failure of issue construction and thus rendered superfluous. *C*'s remainder is not subject to any condition precedent.

158.   F.   *Vested remainder* in fee simple absolute following *C*'s life estate.

159.   F.   *Vested remainder* in a life estate. The condition "if *A* dies before *C*" is superfluous. *A* has a present interest in a life estate, followed by a vested remainder in a life estate in *B*, followed by a vested remainder in a life estate in *C*, followed by a reversion in fee simple absolute in *O*.

160.   D.   *Contingent remainder* in fee simple absolute. The contingency lies in the fact that the heirs are unascertained. *A* has a life estate. *O* retains a reversion despite his express desire. However, the express desire should be sufficient to show a contrary intent to that presumed in the Doctrine of Worthier Title. Therefore, the Doctrine is not applied to give the interest in *O*'s heirs to *O*.

161. *F.   Vested remainder* subject to divestment or, more completely, vested remainder in fee simple subject to executory limitation. The two conditions "when *C* reaches 21, but if *C* dies under 21" appear together and are treated as one condition that is subsequent to *C*'s estate and precedent to *D*'s executory interest. This construction is imposed because of the preference for vested interests.

162. *C.   Life estate.* Before applying the Rule in Shelley's Case, *A* has a legal life estate pur autre vie, *B* has an equitable life estate, the heirs of *B* have a legal contingent remainder in fee simple absolute, and *O* has a reversion. The Rule in Shelley's Case does not apply when the freehold in the ancestor is equitable and the remainder in the heirs is legal.

163. *H.   Fee tail.* The words of limitation are "the heirs of her body." *C*'s interest is a vested remainder following a present interest in *A* in fee tail and a vested remainder in *B* in a life estate.

164. *M.   Fee simple determinable.* The condition subsequent that cuts short *D*'s estate is "as long as *D* remains sober." Since there is no interest designated to take upon the happening of this condition, the interest that fills the gap is a reversionary interest. See problem 165 below. The only two estates that are followed by a reversionary interest are "determinable" and "subject to condition subsequent." Since the condition subsequent is durational ("as long as"), the estate is determinable.

165. *G.   Possibility of Reverter.* The only interest that follows an estate determinable is a possibility of reverter. Since *O* dies at the moment this devise becomes effective, *O* is not able to take this possibility of reverter. Therefore, her heirs inherit her interest.

166. *D.   Contingent remainder* in fee simple absolute. The first condition ("if *B* gets married") is a condition precedent to *B*'s remainder. The second condition ("but if *B* does not get married") is a condition precedent to *C*'s and *D*'s contingent remainders. *C*'s and *D*'s remainders together are alternative to *B*'s remainder.

167. *C.   Reversion* in fee simple absolute. Since there is no vested interest following *A*'s life estate, there is a gap in the conveyance that must be filled with a reversionary interest under the No Gap in Seisin Rule.

168. *B.   Executory interest* in fee simple absolute. The condition ("but if *B* gets married") is a condition subsequent to *B*'s estate and a condition precedent to the interests of *C* and *D*. Since the condition cuts short *B*'s estate to give *C* and *D* vested interests, *C* and *D* have executory interests before the condition occurs. *B* has a vested remainder in fee simple subject to executory limitation.

169. *C.   Life estate. A* has a fee tail, followed by a vested remainder in a life estate in *B*, followed by a contingent remainder in fee simple absolute in *B*'s unborn children and a reversion in *O*. The Modified Rule in Wild's Case operates to divide the interests of *B* and *B*'s children in this way unless *B* has a child before the termination of *A*'s fee tail.

170. *O.   Fee simple subject to executory limitation.* The Modified Rule in Wild's Case operates to give *B* and *X* a tenancy in common in a fee simple estate. Since their vested remainder following *A*'s fee tail is subject to open to admit other children as they are born to *B* (until the class closes by *B*'s death or the termination of *A*'s fee tail), the estate is a fee simple subject to executory limitation.

171. *Q.   None of the above is correct. A* has a present interest in a life estate pur autre vie and a vested remainder in fee tail, followed by *C*'s vested remainder in fee simple absolute. The Merger Rule ordinarily merges a life estate with a fee tail, but the third exception to the Merger Rule suggests that a life estate pur autre vie should not be allowed to merge with a fee tail.

172. *D.   Contingent remainder* in fee simple absolute. The Doctrine of Worthier Title does not apply to a grantor's creation of a future interest in heirs of her body.

173. *I.   None.* The Rule in Shelley's Case converts the interest in the heirs of *A*'s body into an interest in *A* in fee tail. *A* has a present interest in a life estate and a vested remainder in fee tail that merge to form a present interest in fee tail. *O* has a reversion in fee simple absolute.

174. *E.   Life estate determinable. A*'s present interest is not followed by any future interest in a grantee in freehold. The durational condition ("for as long as . . .") makes *A*'s estate determinable. *O* has a reversion in fee simple absolute.

175. *B.   Term of years determinable. B*'s estate is a nonfreehold since it is defined by a set period of time. The durational condition makes *B*'s estate determinable. If *B* ever takes possession of her estate, it will ride piggyback on *O*'s fee simple absolute.

4

Rules to Govern Events Subsequent to the Conveyance

In addition to rules for identification at the time of conveyance, there are rules to determine what happens to the interests in a conveyance upon the happening of certain events. These are described in the five rules below.

A. DESTRUCTIBILITY OF CONTINGENT REMAINDERS

Contingent remainders are destroyed if they do not take immediately upon the termination of all the preceding estates. For example, where O conveys "to A for life and then to B if B gets married," B has a contingent remainder in fee simple absolute, preceded by a present interest in a life estate in A and supported by a reversion in fee simple absolute in O. If B gets married on or before the termination of A's life estate, B's remainder becomes vested and will become a present interest in fee simple absolute upon the termination of A's life estate. If B has not married by the time A's life estate terminates, B's remainder is destroyed at that time. O's reversion then becomes a present interest in fee simple absolute.

If the condition that must be satisfied to vest a remainder on time is birth, it should be remembered that a posthumous child is considered in existence from the time of conception. Thus, if O conveys "to A for life, then to the children of A," and A dies while his wife is pregnant with their first child, the child is entitled to her interest upon birth. The Destructibility Rule does not apply as long as the child is born alive.

Note that the Destructibility Rule applies only to legal contingent remainders in freehold estates. It does not apply to equitable contingent remainders, or to remainders in personal property, or to future interests in a term of years. Note also that many states have abrogated the Destructibility Rule.

B. INDESTRUCTIBILITY OF EXECUTORY INTERESTS

Executory interests are not destroyed if they do not take immediately upon the termination of all the preceding estates. In other words, executory interests do not need preceding estates in grantees to support them. For example, where O conveys "to A for life, but if B gets married then to B," A has a present interest in a life estate subject to executory limitation, B has an executory interest in fee simple absolute, and O has a reversion. If B gets married before the termination of A's life estate, A's life estate is cut short and B's executory interest becomes a present interest in fee simple absolute. If B has not married by the time A's life estate terminates, B's executory interest is preserved, and O's reversion becomes a present interest in fee simple subject to executory limitation. Then, when B gets married, O's estate is cut short and B's executory interest becomes a present interest in fee simple absolute.

Likewise, executory interests are not destroyed if they do not take immediately upon the cutting short of a preceding estate. For example, where O conveys "to A and his heirs until A gets married, then to B when she reaches 21," A has a present interest in fee simple determinable that is cut short when he gets married. O has a possibility of reverter in fee simple subject to executory limitation. B has an executory interest that cuts short O's estate when she becomes 21. If B reaches age 21 before A gets married, A's estate becomes a fee simple subject to executory limitation and B's interest remains an executory interest that will cut short A's estate when A gets married.

If B does not reach 21 by the time A gets married, O's possibility of reverter becomes a present interest in fee simple subject to executory limitation until the time when B reaches 21. If B dies without reaching 21, the condition precedent to B's interest (B's reaching 21) is impossible to fulfill and her executory interest is destroyed by that fact. The condition subsequent to O's estate (B's reaching 21) is eliminated and O is left with a present interest in fee simple absolute. If A never gets married, the possibility of reverter in O and the executory interest in B are destroyed by that fact, and A's estate becomes one in fee simple absolute (inherited by A's heirs upon A's death if A has not conveyed or devised).

C. RULE IN PUREFOY v. ROGERS

A remainder may not transform into an executory interest in order to escape the Destructibility of Contingent Remainders Rule. The Rule in Purefoy v. Rogers (1670) is really a corollary of the Destructibility Rule. For example, where O conveys "to A for life, then to B if B gets married," B has a contingent remainder that cannot transform into an executory interest if B has not married by or at the termination of A's life estate. B's interest is destroyed by the Destructibility of Contingent Remainders Rule and

B loses her interest at that time. Note that there is nothing to prevent an executory interest from transforming into a remainder by reason of subsequent events, or even a remainder from transforming into an executory interest, as long as it is not to escape the Destructibility Rule.

The transformation of an executory interest into a remainder is illustrated by *O*'s conveyance "to *A* and his heirs, but if *A* gets married, then to *B* for life, then to *C*." *A* has a present interest in fee simple subject to executory limitation, and *B* and *C* each have executory interests at the time of the conveyance. If *A* were to get married, *B* then would have a present interest in a life estate and *C* would have a vested remainder in fee simple absolute.

The transformation of a remainder into an executory interest is described in 3 Restatement of Property §278e (Illustration 5), at 1442 (1940):

> 5. *A*, owning Blackacre in fee simple absolute, transfers Blackacre "to *B* for life, remainder to *B*'s children and their heirs, but if *B* has no children alive at the time of his (*B*'s) death, then to *C* and his heirs." *B* has no child when *A* makes this transfer. *C* has a remainder subject to the stated condition precedent. *B* has a son *D*. . . . *D* thereupon acquires a remainder vested subject to complete defeasance and thenceforth *C* has an executory interest.

B has a present interest in a life estate followed by a reversion in *A* in fee simple absolute. *B*'s unborn children have a contingent remainder in fee simple subject to executory limitation. What will sever their interest is the condition subsequent of survivorship to the death of *B*. When *D* is born, *A*'s reversion is divested. *D* has a vested remainder subject to open (the contingent remainder in the unborn children transforming into an executory interest) in fee simple subject to executory limitation (the contingent remainder in *C* transforming into an executory interest).

D. MERGER RULE

See Rule H in Chapter 3 at page 43 above.

E. TRANSFERABILITY

All interests are alienable except, in some jurisdictions, the possibility of reverter, the right of reentry, and the contingent remainder. All interests are devisable unless they are in a fee tail or a life estate (except that a life estate pur autre vie is devisable), and in some jurisdictions, if they are a possibility of reverter or a right of reentry. All interests are inheritable unless they are in a life estate (except that a life estate pur autre vie is inheritable). An interest in a fee tail is inheritable only by issue.

Problem Set IV

The problems in this section ask for a description of an interest or an estate. The answers for interest are:

A. present interest
B. executory interest
C. reversion
D. contingent remainder
E. right of reentry
F. vested remainder
G. possibility of reverter
H. vested remainder subject to open
I. none
J. none of the above is correct

The answers for estate are:

A. term of years
B. term of years determinable
C. life estate
D. life estate pur autre vie
E. life estate determinable
F. life estate subject to condition subsequent
G. life estate subject to executory limitation
H. fee tail
I. fee tail determinable
J. fee tail subject to condition subsequent
K. fee tail subject to executory limitation
L. fee simple absolute
M. fee simple determinable
N. fee simple subject to condition subsequent
O. fee simple subject to executory limitation
P. none
Q. none of the above is correct

Problems

O conveys to *A* for life, then to *A*'s children who shall attain the age of 18 and their heirs, but if *A* dies within the next three years, then to *A*'s children if they reach 18 and their heirs. *B* is an only child of *A* and is two years old at the time of the conveyance. *A* then dies a year later.

176. What is *B*'s interest?
177. What is *O*'s interest?

O conveys to *A* for life, then to *B* for life, then to the children of *D* who survive *D* and their heirs. *C* is *D*'s only child at the time of the conveyance. *A* and *B* die shortly after the conveyance, leaving *C* and *D* surviving them.

178. What is *C*'s interest?
179. What is *O*'s estate?

O conveys to *A* and the heirs of her body, then to *B* and his heirs if *B* has a son. *O* then conveys all interest he has left in the property to *A* and her heirs.

180. What is *A*'s estate?
181. What is *B*'s interest?

O conveys to *A* for life, then, if *B* reaches 18, to *B* and his heirs, but if he has not reached 18 by the time *A* dies, to *B* and his heirs when he does reach 18. *B* is 15 at the time of the conveyance. Five years after the conveyance *A* has not yet died.

182. What is *B*'s interest?

O conveys to *A* and the heirs of her body. *A* then conveys all interest she has in the property to *B* and his heirs.

183. What is *B*'s estate?

O conveys Blackacre to *A* for life. *O* then conveys his remaining interest in Blackacre to *B* for life.

184. What is *B*'s interest?

O conveys to *A* for life, then if *B* gets married, to *B*, but if *B* does not get married, to *C*. *A* conveys her life estate back to *O*.

185. What is *O*'s estate?

O conveys to *A* for life, then to *B* for life, then to the children of *D* who survive *D* and their heirs. *C* is presently *D*'s only child. *A* then conveys any interest he has in the property back to *O*.

186. What is *O*'s interest?
187. What is *C*'s interest?

O conveys to *A* for life, then to *B* for life, then to the children of *D* who survive *D* and their heirs. *C* is *D*'s only child at the time of the conveyance. One year later *A* and *D* die, leaving *B* and *C* still alive. At this point:

188. What is *C*'s interest?

O conveys to *A* for life. *A* then conveys to *B* for ten years, and then to *C*. One year later *A* dies.

189. What is *O*'s estate?

O conveys to *A* and her heirs, but if *A* dies without issue, then to *B* and his heirs. *A* loses her only child in a car accident. One month later, *A* has a heart attack and dies.

190.   What is *B*'s interest?

O conveys to *A* for life, then to *B* and her heirs if *X* gets married. *B* dies, then *X* gets married. *A* is still alive.

191.   What is the interest in *B*'s heirs?

O conveys Blackacre to *A* for life, then to *B* if *B* gets married, but if *B* does not get married, to the heirs of *O*. One day later *O* conveys all his remaining interest in Blackacre to *A*.

192.   What is *A*'s estate?

O conveys Blackacre to *A* for life, then to *B* for life if *B* has a son, then to *C* for life. When it becomes apparent that *B* will not get married, *O* makes a second conveyance to *C* of all his remaining interest in Blackacre.

193.   What is *C*'s interest?

O conveys to *A* for life, then to *O*'s son, *B*, and his heirs. *O* then dies and *B* is his only heir.

194.   What is *B*'s interest?

O conveys to *A* for life, then to the children of *A*. *A* has one child, *X*, at the time of the conveyance. *A* conveys all her interest to *O*.

195.   What is *O*'s estate?

O conveys to *A* for life, then to the children of *A* for the life of the survivor, then to *B*. *A* has one child, *X*, at the time of the conveyance. *A* conveys all her interest to *B*.

196.   What is *B*'s interest?

O conveys Blackacre to *A* and her heirs, but if *A* quits high school, *O* shall have the right to reenter and take Blackacre as of her former estate. *A* quits high school.

197.   What is *O*'s interest?

O conveys to *A* and her heirs, but if *A* gets married, then to *B* for life, then if *C* gets married, to *C* for life. *B* conveys all his interest back to *O*. Then *A* gets married. Then *C* gets married.

198.   What is *C*'s interest?

O conveys Blackacre to *A* for life. *A* then conveys Blackacre to *B* for *B*'s life.

199.   What is *B*'s estate?

O conveys to *A* and her issue, then to *B* for life. *A* then conveys all her interest in the property to *X*. *A* then dies, leaving a son, *C*, surviving her as her only heir. *X* then dies without issue.

200.   What is *B*'s interest?

O conveys to *A* for life as long as *B* does not get married, then to *C* for life. *B* then gets married. *C* then dies.

201.   What is *O*'s estate?

O conveys to *A* for the life of *B*. *A* then conveys all her interest to *C* and her children. *C* has one child, *X*, at the time of *A*'s conveyance.

202.   What is *X*'s interest?

O conveys to *B* for life, then to *C* and the heirs of her body. *C* then dies, leaving only one granddaughter, *X*.

203.   What is *X*'s interest?

O conveys to the children of *A*. *A* has lost all her children by the time of the conveyance, but she has one grandchild, *X*. *A* then bears a child, *M*.

204.   What is *M*'s interest?

O conveys to *A* for life, then to the children of *A*. *A* then forfeits her life estate. Three years later *A* bears her first child, *X*.

205.   What is *X*'s interest?

O conveys to *A* and his heirs until *A* gets married, then to *B* if *B* reaches 21. *A* gets married when *B* is 18 years old.

206.   What is *B*'s interest?

O conveys to *A* and his heirs, but if *A* dies without issue, then to *B*. Two years later *A*'s wife bears *A*'s first child, *X*. *X* then dies. *A* then dies.

207.   What is *B*'s interest?

O conveys to *A* for life, then, if *B* gets married, to *B* for life, otherwise to *C*. *A* then conveys all her interest in the property to *C*.

208.   What is *C*'s interest?

O conveys to *A* for life, then, if *B* gets married, to *B* and his heirs, otherwise to *C*. *A* then conveys all her interest in the property to *C*.

209.   What is *C*'s interest?

O conveys to *A* for life, then, if *B* gets married, to *B* for life, otherwise to *A*'s heirs. *B* then gets married. *A* then conveys all her interest in the property to *C*.

210.   What is *C*'s interest?

O conveys to *A* for life, then, if *B* gets married, to *B* for life, otherwise to *A*'s heirs. *A* then conveys all interest in the property to *C*. *B* then gets married.

211.   What is *C*'s interest?

O conveys to *A* for life, then, if *B* gets married, to *B*, and if *B* does not get married, to *C*. *O* then dies without a will, leaving *A* as his only heir. *B* is unmarried.

212.   What is *C*'s interest?

O conveys to *A* and her children. At the time of the conveyance, *A* has no children. Two years later *A* has her first child, *B*. *A* then conveys all her interest to *O*.

213.   What is *O*'s estate?

O conveys to *A* for 100 years if she should live so long, then to *A*'s husband, *B*, for life, then to trustees for the life of *B* in trust for *B* for life and to preserve contingent remainders, then in fee simple to the children of *A* and *B* who should survive *A* and *B*. *B* then dies.

214.   What is *A*'s estate?
215.   What is the interest of the children of *A* and *B*?

O conveys to *A* for life, then, if *B* reaches 18, to *B* and his heirs, but if he has not reached 18 by the time *A* dies, to *B* and his heirs when he does reach 18. *B* is 15 at the time of the conveyance. Two years after the conveyance, *A* dies.

216.   What is *B*'s interest?

O conveys to *A* for life, then to *B*'s first son and his heirs. *A* dies. *B*'s first son, *X*, is born to *B*'s wife one month after *A*'s death.

217.   What is *X*'s interest?

O conveys to *A* and his heirs, but if *A* gets married, then to *B* for life, then to *C* for life, then to the heirs of *C*. *A* gets married.

218.   What is *C*'s interest?

O conveys to *A* for ten years. One year later, *A* conveys her interest to *B* for life. Then *O* dies, leaving *H* as his only heir. Then *A* dies, leaving *X* as his only heir.

219.   What is *B*'s estate?

O conveys to *A* for life, then to *B* and his heirs. *B* then conveys to *O* as long as *B* does not get married. *O* dies, leaving *X* as his only heir. Then *A* dies. *B* is still unmarried.

220.   What is *B*'s interest?

O conveys Blackacre to *A* for life, and if *A* dies without issue, to *B* and his heirs. *A* then conveys her interest in Blackacre to *C* and his heirs. *A* then marries *D* and has a son, *E*. *A* then dies, devising all her interest in Blackacre to *F*.

221. What is *F*'s interest?

O conveys Blackacre to *A* for life, then one year after the termination of *A*'s estate, to such of *A*'s children as attain the age of 15. At the time of the conveyance, *A* has two twin children, *B* and *C*, who are each 13 years old. Two years later, *B* and *C* reach 15. Then *A* has another child, *D*. Then *B* dies, devising all his interest to *X*. Then *A* dies, devising all her interest to *X*. Then, several years later, *D* reaches 15 with *C* still alive.

222. What is *D*'s interest?

O conveys Blackacre to *A* for life, then one day later to the children of *B*. *A* dies. Two years later, *B* has her first child, *X*. One year later, *B* has a second child, *Y*, and *B* dies in childbirth.

223. What is *Y*'s interest?

O conveys Blackacre to *A* for life, then to the children of *B*. *A* dies. Then two years later *B* has her first child, *X*. One year after that, *B* has a second child, *Y*, and *B* dies in childbirth.

224. What is *X*'s interest?

O conveys Blackacre to *A* for life, then to *B* and the heirs of his body, then to *C* and his heirs. *A*, *B*, and *C* are killed in a car crash, each leaving a son (*D*, *E*, and *F* respectively) as his only heir. The three sons are killed in a plane crash, each childless, each leaving a spouse (*X*, *Y*, and *Z* respectively) as his only heir.

225. What is *Y*'s interest?

O conveys to *A* for life, then to *A*'s widow for life, then to the issue of *A*. Two years later, *O* sells any remaining interest he has in the property to *A*. One year later, *A*'s wife dies; two weeks later, *A* dies from grief, leaving his only son, *M*, surviving him. *A* also has left a will in which all his property is devised to his friend, *P*.

226. What is *P*'s interest?
227. What is *M*'s estate?

O conveys to *A* for life, then, if *B* gets married, to *B* and the heirs of her body. Two months later, *A* dies devising her interest, if any, to *X*. *B* is still unmarried.

228. What is *O*'s interest?

O conveys to *A* and her heirs until *A* gets married, then to the heirs of *O*. *O* dies, leaving a will in which he devises all his property to *X*. *O* has one living relative at the time of his death, his son, *S*.

229. What is *X*'s interest?

O conveys to *A* for ten years, then to *B* for life. *B* dies one year later, leaving *H* as his only heir. Then *A* dies, leaving *S* as his only heir.

    230.   What is *S*'s estate?

O devises to *A* for life, then to *B* for 30 years, then to *C* and the heirs of his body as long as the property is used as a farm. The next year *A* and *B* die, leaving *H* and *S* as their respective heirs.

    231.   What is *C*'s estate?

O conveys to *A* and her children. At the time of this conveyance, *A* has no children. One day later, *O* conveys all interest he has remaining in Blackacre to *A*. Two years later, *A* dies while giving birth to her only child, *B*. In her will, *A* leaves all her property to X.

    232.   What is *B*'s interest?

O conveys to *A* for life, then to *B* if *B* places a red rose on *A*'s grave each year at Christmas for the first five Christmases after her death. Then *A* dies, and *B* places a red rose on her grave the next Christmas.

    233.   What is *B*'s interest?

O conveys to *A* and *A*'s children, but if *A* dies without issue, then to B. *A* has children, *X* and *Y*, at the time of the conveyance. Then *X* has a son, *S*, and *Y* has a daughter, *D*. Then *X* and *Y* die, leaving *S* and *D* respectively as their only heirs. Then *A* dies, devising all her interest to *T*.

    234.   What is *S*'s estate?

O conveys to *A* for life, then to *B* and the heirs of his body, if *B* gets married, but if *B* does not get married, to *C* for life. *O* then conveys any remaining interest in the property to *A*. Then *B* gets married.

    235.   What is *A*'s interest?

O conveys to *A* so long as she lives and maintains the property, but if she fails to maintain the property, then *O* shall have the right to reenter and retake the property as of his former estate. *O* dies leaving *H* as his only heir. *A* fails to maintain the property. Then *A* dies leaving *M* as her only heir.

    236.   What is *M*'s interest?

O conveys to *A* and his issue by his wife, *W*, then to *B* if *B* has a son. *W* dies without ever having had issue. *A* marries *X*. Then *O* conveys any remaining interest he has in the property to *A* and his issue by his wife, *X*. Two years later, *B*'s first son, *Y*, is born. *A*'s first son, *Z*, is born shortly thereafter, and *X* dies in childbirth. Then *A* dies.

    237.   What is *Y*'s interest?
    238.   What is *Z*'s interest?
    239.   What is *O*'s interest?

O conveys to *A* for life. Then *A* conveys to *B* for life. Then *B* conveys to *C* for ten years.

    240.   What is *B*'s estate?
    241.   What is *A*'s interest?

O devises to *A* and her heirs, but if *A* ever goes to jail, then *O* may reenter and possess the premises as of his former estate. *O*'s heirs are *X* and *Y*. After *O*'s death, *A* goes to jail.

    242.   What is *A*'s estate?

O conveys to *A* for life, then to the children of *B*. At the time of the conveyance, *B* has no children. Thereafter, *B* has a child, *X*. *X* dies when she is one month old, leaving *B* as her only heir.

    243.   What is *B*'s interest?

O conveys to *A* for life, then to *B* and his heirs, but if *X* dies without issue, then to *C* and his heirs. *X* dies without issue living at his death.

    244.   What is *C*'s interest?

O conveys Blackacre to *A* for life, then to *B* and his heirs if *B* gets married, but to *C* and his heirs if *B* does not get married. *O* then conveys Whiteacre to *A* for life, then to *B* and his heirs, but, if *B* does not get married, then to *C* and his heirs. *A* dies. Then *B* gets married.

    245.   What is *B*'s interest in Blackacre?
    246.   What is *B*'s interest in Whiteacre?

O conveys to *A* and his issue, then to the issue of *B* who survive *B*. *B* bears her first child, *X*. Then *A* dies without issue.

    247.   What is *X*'s interest?

O devises to *A* for life, then to *B* if *B* gets married. *A* conveys all her interest in the property to *X*. *B* gets married. Then *A* dies. At the time of *O*'s death, *A* was *O*'s only heir. At the time of *A*'s death, *B* is *A*'s only heir.

    248.   What is *X*'s estate?
    249.   What is *B*'s interest?

O conveys to *A* for life, then to the heirs of *B*, but if *M* ever goes to law school, then the property, no matter who owns it, shall automatically revert to *O* and his heirs. *A* dies, leaving *X* as her only heir. Then *O* dies leaving *Y* as his only heir. Then *B* dies, leaving *Z* as his only heir.

    250.   What is *Y*'s estate?

O conveys to *A* for life, then to the heirs of *B*, but if *M* ever goes to law school, then the property, no matter who owns it, shall automatically revert to *O* and his heirs. *B* dies, leaving *Z* as his only heir. Then *A* dies, leaving *X* as her only heir. Then *O* dies, leaving *Y* as his only heir.

251.   What is *Y*'s interest?

O conveys Blackacre to *A* for life, then to the children of *A* for the life of the survivor, then to the heirs of *A*. *A* dies leaving his pregnant spouse, *S*, as his only heir. *A*'s will gives all of *A*'s interest in Blackacre to *M*. Six months later, *A*'s only child, *X*, is born.

252.   What is *M*'s interest?

O conveys Blackacre to *A* for life, then to *O*'s heirs. *O* sells Blackacre to *X* and then dies, leaving *H* as his only heir.

253.   What is *H*'s interest?

O conveys to *A* for life, then to *B* and his issue if he gets married on or before the termination of *A*'s life estate, otherwise to *B* and his issue if he gets married afterwards. *A* dies and one month later *B* gets married. One year later *B* dies, leaving his spouse, *S*, and his son, *T*, as his only heirs.

254.   What is *T*'s interest?

O conveys to *A* for life, then to the children of *B* and their heirs, but if any of *B*'s children dies before the time of *B*'s death, then to *C* and his heirs. Two years after the conveyance, *B* has his first child, *X*.

255.   What is *X*'s interest?
256.   What is *X*'s estate?

O conveys Blackacre to *A* and his heirs, but if *A* dies childless, then *O* shall have the right to reenter and take the property as of his former estate. Two years later, *A* dies childless and leaves his grandson, *S*, as his only heir.

257.   What is *S*'s estate?

O conveys to *A* for life, then to the children of *B*. *B* has one child, *X*, who is 20 years old. Two years later, *X* dies, leaving all his property to *H*. One year later, *A* dies. Three years later, *B* has another child, *Y*.

258.   What is *Y*'s estate?

O conveys to *A* for life, then to *B*, but if *B* gets married, then to *C* for life, then to *D* and his issue. *O* dies and wills all his property to *B*. Then *B* gets married.

259.   What is *B*'s interest?

O conveys to *A* for life, then to *B* for life, then to *C* for life if *C* gets married, then to the heirs of *B*. *B* dies, leaving *X* as her only heir. Then *C* gets married.

260.   What is *X*'s interest?

O conveys Blackacre to *A* and his issue, then, if *B* gets married, to *B*, and if *B* does not get married, to *O*'s heirs. *O* then dies and wills any remaining interest in Blackacre to *A*'s children. *O*'s heir is *X*. *A*'s issue at the time of *O*'s conveyance and at the time of *O*'s will are two children, *J* and *K*. Then *A* dies. Then *B* gets married.

261. What is *X*'s interest?
262. What is *B*'s interest?
263. What is *J*'s estate?

O conveys Blackacre to *A* as long as Blackacre is used as a farm. *A* conveys Blackacre to *B*, but, if *B* gets married, *A* shall have the right to reenter and retake Blackacre as of her former estate.

264. What is *A*'s interest?
265. What is *A*'s estate?

O conveys Blackacre to *A* and her heirs, but, if *A* dies without issue, then to *B* for life, then, no earlier than one day after the death of *B*, to *C* and her issue, then to *D*. *O* conveys any remaining interest in Blackacre to *B*. Then *A* bears her first child, *X*.

266. What is *D*'s interest?

O conveys Blackacre to *A* for life, then to *B*. *O* sells Blackacre to *X* and then dies, leaving *B* as his only heir.

267. What is *B*'s interest?

O conveys to *A* for life, and, if *B* gets married, then to *B*, but if *B* flunks the first-year property course in law school, then to *C*, and, if *B* does not get married, the property shall revert to *O*. *B* flunks the first-year property course in law school and then gets married.

268. What is *C*'s interest?

O conveys to *A* for life, then to *B* for life if *B* gets married, then, if *B* gets married, either to *A*'s heirs if *C* gets married or to *D* if *C* does not get married. *C* gets married.

269. What is *A*'s interest?

O conveys Blackacre to *A* for life, then to *B* for ten years, then to *C* and the heirs of her body, but, if *C* uses Blackacre as a tavern, then to *D* and his heirs. *C* dies, leaving her son, *X*, as her only heir.

270. What is *X*'s interest?
271. What is *X*'s estate?

O conveys to *A* for life, then one day later to *B* for life, then to *C* for ten years, then to *D* if *D* gets married. *A* dies, and a week passes.

272. What is *D*'s interest?

O conveys to *A* for her life or for the life of the last of her children to survive, whichever is longer, then to *B* and her issue, if *B* gets married. Then *A*'s only child living at the time of *O*'s conveyance dies.

273.   What is *A*'s estate?
274.   What is *B*'s interest?

O conveys Blackacre to *A* and her heirs as long as Blackacre is used as a farm. Then *O* conveys any interest he has remaining in Blackacre to *B* for life. *B* then conveys to *C* for *C*'s life.

275.   What is *C*'s interest?

Answers

176.   *B.   Executory interest* in fee simple absolute. *O* conveys two interests to *A*'s children, a contingent remainder following *A*'s life estate (and accompanying *O*'s reversion) and an executory interest to cut short *O*'s reversion. The remainder is contingent on reaching the age of 18; the executory interest is contingent on reaching 18 and on *A*'s dying within the next three years. When *A* dies, the contingent remainder is destroyed by the Destructibility of Contingent Remainders Rule. The executory interest is the only one left in *B*. It is not destroyed (Indestructibility of Executory Interests) but must await the occurrence of the condition precedent ("if they reach 18") before it becomes a present interest.

177.   *A.   Present interest* in fee simple subject to executory limitation. In the gap after *A*'s life estate, *O* retained a reversion, which is now a present interest.

178.   *I.   None.* By the conveyance, *A* receives a present interest in a life estate, *B* receives a vested remainder in a life estate, the children of *D* receive a contingent remainder in fee simple absolute, and *O* retains a reversion in fee simple absolute. The condition of survivorship is not satisfied at the time the preceding estates terminate, and, therefore, the children's contingent remainder is destroyed by the Destructibility of Contingent Remainders Rule. If *A* alone had died or *B* alone had died, the contingent remainder would still be supported by a preceding estate.

179.   *L.   Fee simple absolute.* *O*'s reversion at the time of the conveyance has now become a present interest.

180.   *Q.   None of the above is correct.* The conveyance gives *A* a present interest in fee tail, *B* a contingent remainder in fee simple absolute, and *O* a reversion. *O* conveys his reversion to *A*. It does not merge with *A*'s present interest because of the exception to the Merger Rule, that is, a fee simple does not merge with a fee tail. Therefore, *A* now has a present estate in fee tail plus a reversion in fee simple.

181.   *D.   Contingent remainder* in fee simple absolute. This remainder is saved because *A*'s vested interests cannot merge.

182.   *F.   Vested remainder* in fee simple absolute. When the condition of reaching 18 was satisfied, the contingent remainder became vested. The condition precedent to the executory interest (*B*'s not reaching 18 by the time *A* dies) will never happen. The ex-

ecutory interest is thus destroyed. (Note that executory interests may be destroyed by the failure of their conditions precedent ever to happen — not by the failure of their conditions precedent to happen upon the termination of preceding estates.)

183.   D.   *Life estate pur autre vie.* O's conveyance gives A a present interest in fee tail, and O retains a reversion in fee simple absolute. A's conveyance gives B the estate that A had in effect. It is not called a fee tail because B's issue do not inherit it. B will lose this estate when A dies, and it will pass to A's issue by descent. The estate in A's issue is called a fee tail because their issue will inherit it.

184.   C.   *Reversion* in a life estate. O retains a reversion in himself with the first conveyance, and he conveys a life estate to B in this reversion in the second conveyance. At that point, A has a life estate, B has a reversion in a life estate, and O has a reversion in fee simple absolute to follow B's estate.

185.   L.   *Fee simple absolute.* Upon the conveyance, A has a present interest in a life estate, followed by a reversion in fee simple absolute in O. B and C have alternative contingent remainders. When A conveys to O, O takes a life estate pur autre vie. The merger of this life estate pur autre vie with O's reversion in fee simple absolute causes the destruction of the contingent remainders in B and C.

186.   J.   *None of the above is correct.* Upon the conveyance, A has a life estate, B has a vested remainder for life, the children of D (including C) have a contingent remainder in fee simple absolute, and O has a reversion. A's conveyance to O does not cause a merger because B's vested interest cannot be merged out. O has a present interest in a life estate pur autre vie plus a reversion in fee simple absolute.

187.   D.   *Contingent remainder* in fee simple absolute. This interest is saved from merger by the presence of B's vested interest.

188.   F.   *Vested remainder* in fee simple absolute. At the time of the conveyance, A has a life estate, B has a vested remainder in a life estate, D's children have a contingent remainder in fee simple absolute, and O has a reversion in fee simple absolute. When A and D die, B is left with a present interest for life. C's vested remainder in fee simple absolute is not subject to open because no other child of D can be born (class closes).

189.   L.   *Fee simple absolute.* O conveyed a present interest in a life estate to A and retained a reversion in fee simple absolute. A then conveyed to C a life estate pur autre vie subject to a term of years determinable in B. When A dies, the term of years as well as the life estate pur autre vie terminates. (A could not convey more than she had.) O's reversion becomes a present interest.

190.   A.   *Present interest* in fee simple absolute. Upon the conveyance, A has a present interest in fee simple subject to executory limitation. B has an executory interest in fee simple absolute. The words "dies without issue" are given a definite failure of issue construction. A died without issue even though

she had had issue. Therefore, the condition precedent to *B*'s taking a present interest is satisfied and *A*'s estate is cut off.

191.   *F.   Vested remainder* in fee simple absolute. Upon the conveyance, *B* has a contingent remainder, following *A*'s present interest in a life estate and accompanying *O*'s reversion in fee simple absolute. *B* does not have to be alive when *X* gets married in order to satisfy the condition precedent. *B*'s heirs inherited *B*'s contingent remainder, which then became vested when *X* married.

192.   *L.   Fee simple absolute.* Upon *O*'s first conveyance, *A* has a present interest in a life estate, *B* has a contingent remainder in fee simple absolute, and *O* has a reversion in fee simple absolute. The preference for vesting exception does not apply because the condition (*B* getting married) is not an age contingency. *O* appears to have conveyed an alternative contingent remainder to the heirs of *O*, but the Doctrine of Worthier Title construes this conveyance as a reversion in *O* himself. *O* then conveys this reversion to *A*. It merges with *A*'s life estate and destroys the intervening contingent remainder in *B*.

193.   *F.   Vested remainder* in fee simple absolute. Upon the first conveyance, *A* has a life estate, *B* has a contingent remainder in a life estate accompanying *C*'s vested remainder in a life estate, and *O* has a reversion. Upon the second conveyance, *C* receives *O*'s reversion, which merges with *C*'s vested remainder. *B*'s contingent remainder is still supported by *A*'s life estate and accompanies *C*'s vested remainder.

194.   *F.   Vested remainder* in fee simple absolute. The Doctrine of Worthier Title does not apply because the interest in remainder is not to "heirs" but rather to a specific person, *B*. *O*'s death has no effect on the ownerships.

195.   *D.   Life estate pur autre vie.* Upon the conveyance, *A* has a life estate, the unborn children of *A* have an executory interest in fee simple absolute, and *X* has a vested remainder subject to open in a fee simple absolute. *A*'s conveyance gives *O* a life estate for the life of *A*. Note that the Rule in Shelley's Case does not apply when the remainder is to "children."

196.   *Q.   None of the above is correct.* *B* has a present interest in a life estate pur autre vie plus a vested remainder in fee simple absolute. Upon the conveyance, *A* has a life estate, *X* has a vested remainder subject to open in a life estate pur autre vie, the unborn children of *A* have an executory interest in a life estate pur autre vie, and *B* has a vested remainder in fee simple absolute. *A*'s conveyance gives *B* a life estate pur autre vie. This vested interest does not merge with *B*'s vested remainder because of the intervening vested interest in X.

197.   *E.   Right of reentry* in fee simple absolute. Upon the conveyance, *A* has a fee simple subject to condition subsequent and *O* has a right of reentry. When the condition subsequent occurs, *O* has the power to terminate *A*'s estate, but that power must be exercised before *A*'s estate is terminated. It has not yet been exercised here.

198. *I. None.* At the time of the conveyance, *A* has a fee simple subject to executory limitation, *B* has an executory interest in a life estate, *C* has an executory interest in a life estate, and *O* retains a reversionary interest. *B's* conveyance gives *O* an executory interest in a life estate pur autre vie in addition to *O's* reversionary interest. (Could merger occur in this situation to merge out *C's* executory interest?) When the condition subsequent (*A's* marriage) occurs, *A's* estate is divested, and *O's* interest transforms into a present interest in a life estate pur autre vie plus a reversion in fee simple absolute. *C's* interest would transform into a contingent remainder for life, but the Merger Rule combines *O's* two vested interests, merging out *C's* contingent remainder and leaving *O* with a present interest in fee simple absolute. *C* gets married too late to save his interest.

199. *D. Life estate pur autre vie.* Since *A* specified "for *B's* life," the estate in *B* is a life estate for the life of *A* or *B*, whoever dies first (life estate pur autre vie). If *B* dies before *A*, the interest will revert to *A*. If *A* dies before *B*, the interests of both *A* and *B* are terminated and *O's* reversion becomes a present interest. On the other hand, if *A* had merely specified "to *B*" in her conveyance, *B* would have had a life estate for the life of *A*.

200. *F. Vested remainder* in a life estate. Upon the conveyance, *A* has a present interest in fee tail, *B* has a vested remainder in a life estate, and *O* has a reversion in fee simple absolute. *X's* interest in the fee tail estate lasts only for the life of *A* (and may be called a life estate pur autre vie). *A's* son, *C*, inherits the fee tail upon *A's* death. *X's* death without issue is irrelevant.

201. *L. Fee simple absolute.* Upon the conveyance, *A* has a present interest in a life estate subject to executory limitation, *C* has a vested remainder in a life estate (ready to follow the natural termination of *A's* life estate, if not sooner through *B's* marriage), and *O* has a reversion in fee simple absolute. *B's* marriage transforms *C's* vested remainder into a present interest in a life estate. This life estate ends with the death of *C*, and *O's* reversion transforms into a present interest in fee simple absolute.

202. *A. Present interest* in a life estate pur autre vie shared as a one-half undivided share with *C*. Under the Modified Rule in Wild's Case, *C* and *X* share a tenancy in common in the life estate pur autre vie conveyed by *A*. *O* has a reversion in fee simple absolute.

203. *F. Vested remainder* in a fee tail. *C's* vested remainder in fee tail is inherited by *X* when *C* dies. Note that *X* takes her interest as an heir from *C*, not as a purchaser from *O*. *B* has a present interest in a life estate. *O* has a reversion in fee simple absolute.

204. *A. Present interest* subject to open in a fee simple absolute. Since the time for distribution to the class of children is immediate and there are no takers at the time of *O's* conveyance, the Rule of Convenience does not operate to close the class. The class will close only upon the death of *A*. Upon *O's* convey-

ance, *O* retains a present interest in fee simple subject to executory limitation, and *A*'s children have an executory interest in fee simple absolute. When *M* is born, her interest vests in possession, but it does not close the class. *A*'s unborn children continue to have an executory interest in fee simple absolute.

205.   *I.   None.* *A*'s children have a contingent remainder (following *A*'s life estate and accompanying *O*'s reversion) that fails to vest before the termination of *A*'s life estate. It is destroyed by the Destructibility of Contingent Remainders Rule. *O* now has a present interest in fee simple absolute.

206.   *B.   Executory interest* in fee simple absolute. Upon *O*'s conveyance, *A* has a present interest in fee simple determinable, *O* has a possibility of reverter in fee simple subject to executory limitation, and *B* has an executory interest in fee simple absolute. *A*'s marriage cuts short *A*'s estate, but the age contingency that is a condition precedent to the vesting of *B*'s estate has not yet occurred. Since executory interests are indestructible, *B*'s interest is not destroyed. *O* has a present interest in fee simple subject to executory limitation.

207.   *A.   Present interest* in fee simple absolute. Upon *O*'s conveyance, *A* has a present interest in fee simple subject to executory limitation, and *B* has an executory interest in fee simple absolute. The die-without-issue condition is given a definite failure of issue construction because it follows a fee simple estate. Although *A* had issue, he did not have issue at his death. Therefore, the condition is satisfied and *A*'s estate is cut short at his death in favor of *B*.

208.   *A.   Present interest* in fee simple absolute. *C* receives a vested remainder in fee simple absolute by *O*'s conveyance and a vested present interest in a life estate pur autre vie by *A*'s conveyance. These interests, created in *C* at different times and back to back, are merged, merging out the contingent remainder in a life estate in *B*.

209.   *J.   None of the above is correct.* Upon *O*'s conveyance, *A* has a present interest in a life estate, *B* and *C* each have alternative contingent remainders in fee simple absolute, and *O* has a reversion in fee simple absolute. *C* cannot have a vested remainder because it would be subject to divestment by *B*'s contingent remainder, a situation that is not allowed. *C* receives a present interest in a life estate pur autre vie by *A*'s conveyance. There is no merger between *C*'s present interest and *C*'s contingent remainder.

210.   *J.   None of the above is correct.* Upon *O*'s conveyance, *A* has a present interest in a life estate and, with the application of the Rule in Shelley's Case, a vested remainder in fee simple absolute. *B* has a contingent remainder in a life estate. Although *A*'s interests are vested in the same person and back to back, there is no merger because of the exception to merger that occurs when the vested interests are created in one person at the same time the contingent remainder is created. When *B* gets

married, *B*'s contingent remainder transforms into a vested remainder. At this point, *A*'s vested interests are no longer back to back. When *A* conveys to *C*, *C* receives a present interest in a life estate pur autre vie and a vested remainder in fee simple absolute. There is no merger because of the intervening vested remainder in *B*.

211. *A.   Present interest* in fee simple absolute. Upon *O*'s conveyance, *A* and *B* have the same interests as mentioned in problem 210 above. The exception to the merger rule no longer exists when *A* conveys her two back to back vested interests to *C*. The two interests are merged, merging out *B*'s contingent remainder. *B*'s later marriage is to no avail.

212. *I.   None.* Upon *O*'s conveyance, *A* has a present interest in a life estate, *B* and *C* each have an alternative contingent remainder in fee simple absolute, and *O* has a reversion in fee simple absolute. *A* receives *O*'s reversion by inheritance and the reversion merges with *A*'s vested present interest, merging out the contingent remainders of *B* and *C*. Upon *A*'s inheritance, *A* has a present interest in fee simple absolute. Note that the condition precedent to *C*'s contingent remainder is not yet satisfied even though *B* is unmarried. The condition is the failure to marry by the termination of *A*'s life estate, which has not occurred at the time of *O*'s death.

213. *D.   Life estate pur autre vie.* The Modified Rule in Wild's Case gives *A* a life estate and *A*'s unborn children a contingent remainder upon *O*'s conveyance. Upon birth, *B* takes a vested remainder subject to open. *A*'s unborn children now have an executory interest in fee simple absolute.

214. *B.   Terms of years determinable.* *A*'s life is the determining condition.

215. *I.   None.* Upon *O*'s conveyance, *B* has a present interest in a life estate subject to a term of years determinable in *A*, the trustees have a vested remainder in a life estate pur autre vie (for the life of *B*), the children of *A* and *B* have a contingent remainder in fee simple absolute, and *O* has a reversion in fee simple absolute. Upon *B*'s death, the vested remainder in *B* and the vested remainder in the trustees terminate. The remainder in the children is contingent on survivorship of both parents and thus does not become vested upon the death of *B*. This contingent remainder is destroyed by the Destructibility of Contingent Remainders Rule since there is no preceding freehold estate left to support it. This is a classic case of a botched conveyance and appears as a problem in A. J. Casner & W. B. Leach, Cases and Text on Property at 327-328 (3d ed. 1984), citing the English case of Cunliffe v. Brancker (1876). This conveyance was designed to preserve the contingent remainders if *B* forfeited his estate. As it turned out, not enough was done. The future interest in the children would have been preserved from destruction if the trustees had been given a life estate for the lives of both *A* and *B*. The trustees' estate then

would have supported the children's remainder until the condition precedent was satisfied, even if *A*'s and *B*'s estates were both forfeited before the ends of their lives. The future interest in the children also would have been preserved from destruction if both *A* and *B* had been given terms of years determinable, that is, "*O* conveys to *A* for 100 years if she should so long live, then to *B* for 100 years if he should so long live, then in fee simple to the children of *A* and *B* who should survive *A* and *B*." The children would have had an executory interest (the present interest in freehold being in *O*), and whether *A* or *B* had died or both forfeited their estates before death, the executory interest would not have been destroyed. It would have ripened into a present interest in fee simple absolute upon the deaths of both *A* and *B* if there had been surviving children.

216.   *B.   Executory interest* in fee simple absolute. *B* has two future interests at the time of the conveyance: (1) a contingent remainder following *A*'s present interest in a life estate and accompanying *O*'s reversion, and (2) an executory interest prepared to cut short *O*'s reversion on the happening of the condition subsequent ("but if he has not reached 18 by the time *A* dies"). The death of *A* destroys *B*'s contingent remainder. *O*'s interest becomes a present interest in fee simple subject to executory limitation until *B* reaches 18. The alternative limitations in this conveyance are one means of avoiding the Rule in Purefoy v. Rogers.

217.   *A.   Present interest* in fee simple absolute. Upon *O*'s conveyance, *A* has a present interest in a life estate, *B*'s unborn son has a contingent remainder in fee simple absolute, and *O* has a reversion in fee simple absolute. A posthumous child is considered to be in existence prior to his birth. The Destructibility of Contingent Remainders Rule does not operate here. If the son were not born alive, the Destructibility Rule would operate to destroy the contingent remainder.

218.   *F.   Vested remainder* in fee simple absolute. At the time of the conveyance, *A* has a fee simple subject to executory limitation, *B* has an executory interest for life, *C* has an executory interest for life, the heirs of *C* have an executory interest for life, and *O* has a reversionary interest. When *A* gets married, the condition subsequent divests *A*'s estate. *B* then has a present interest in a life estate and, before application of the Rule in Shelley's Case, *C* has a vested remainder for life and *C*'s heirs have a contingent remainder in fee simple absolute. The Rule operates upon *A*'s marriage to give *C* a vested remainder in fee simple absolute in place of the remainder in *C*'s heirs. The Merger Rule combines the two interests in *C* to give *C* a vested remainder in fee simple absolute to follow *B*'s present interest. Note that the freehold of the ancestor in the Rule in Shelley's Case need not be in a present interest, and the Rule may operate on a delayed basis.

219.   *B.   Term of years determinable. A* has a term of years that she conveys to *B* to determine upon *B*'s death. The deaths of *O* and

A do not affect the interest in *B*. Upon *O*'s death, *O*'s present interest in fee simple absolute descends to his heir, *H*.

220. *G. Possibility of reverter* in fee simple absolute. *O* conveyed a life estate to *A* and a vested remainder in fee simple absolute to *B*. *B* conveyed a vested remainder in fee simple determinable to *O* and kept the rest of the vested remainder as a possibility of reverter in himself. One might call this interest a possibility of reverter within a vested remainder. *O*'s vested remainder in fee simple determinable is inherited by *X* upon *O*'s death. When *A* dies, the vested remainder becomes a present interest in *X* in fee simple determinable. Whenever *B* gets married, *B* will take a present interest in fee simple absolute. Note that if *O* had conveyed "to *A* for life, then to *B* and his heirs if *B* gets married," *B* would have had a contingent remainder that would have been destroyed under the Destructibility of Contingent Remainders Rule when *A* died before *B* got married.

221. *I. None.* *O*'s conveyance gives *A* a life estate and *B* a contingent remainder, leaving a reversion in *O*. *A* conveys her interest to *C* as a present interest in a life estate pur autre vie (for the life of *A*). When *A* dies, her estate, which is then in *C*, ends. The condition precedent to *B*'s interest is not satisfied, and *B*'s contingent remainder is destroyed. *O*'s reversion transforms into a present interest in fee simple absolute.

222. *A. Present interest* in fee simple absolute shared as an undivided one-third interest in a tenancy in common. Upon *O*'s conveyance, *A* has a life estate, *O* has a reversion in fee simple subject to executory limitation, and *A*'s children have a springing executory interest in fee simple absolute. The class of children is open to include all children alive between the time of the conveyance and the time of *A*'s death plus one year, when the class closes. *B*, *C*, and *D* are included in the class. Since all these children satisfy the condition precedent (reaching 15), they or their heirs are entitled to shares in the estate. When *B* and *C* reach 15, they need to satisfy only one condition precedent (one year passage of time after *A*'s life estate) while the other children still need to satisfy two. When *B* dies, *X* takes his share in the executory interest. When *A* dies, *O* takes a present interest in fee simple subject to executory limitation. *B*'s heir, *X*, and *C* take in possession one-third undivided shares in a present interest in fee simple absolute one year after *A* dies, and *D* receives her share upon reaching 15.

223. *A. Present interest* in fee simple absolute shared as a one-half undivided interest in a tenancy in common. Upon *O*'s conveyance, *A* has a present interest in a life estate, *O* has a reversion in fee simple subject to executory limitation, and *B*'s children have an executory interest in fee simple absolute. There are two conditions subsequent on *O*'s estate: the passage of one day from the termination of *A*'s life estate and the birth of each child. On *A*'s death *O* takes a present interest in fee simple subject to executory limitation. Since there were no members of the class alive at the time designated in the conveyance for

distribution (one day after *A*'s death), the class may close only naturally upon *B*'s death. When *X* is born, she takes a present interest subject to open in fee simple absolute, that is, subject to partial divestment of half the estate in favor of *Y* when he is born.

224. *I.   None.* Upon *O*'s conveyance, *A* has a life estate, *B*'s children have a contingent remainder, and *O* has a reversion. When *A* dies, the children of *B* are as yet unborn. Therefore, the Destructibility of Contingent Remainders Rule operates to destroy the contingent remainder in the children on *A*'s death. *O* now has a present interest in fee simple absolute.

225. *I.   None.* When *A* dies, *A*'s life estate terminates. When *B*'s son dies and there are no more issue, *B*'s fee tail, which was inherited by *E*, terminates. *C*'s vested remainder in fee simple absolute, which was inherited by *F*, becomes a present interest in fee simple absolute inherited by *Z* upon the deaths of *E* and *F*.

226. *C.   Reversion* in fee simple absolute. At the time of the conveyance, *A* has a life estate, *A*'s widow has a contingent remainder in a life estate (she is unascertained), *A* has a vested remainder in fee tail (upon application of the Rule in Shelley's Case), and *O* has a reversion. There is no merger between *A*'s two vested interests because of the exception to the Merger Rule dealing with an intervening contingent remainder. When *O* sells his interest to *A*, *A* has a reversion following his vested remainder in fee tail. There is no merger between the vested remainder and the reversion because of the exception to the Merger Rule dealing with a fee tail. The death of *A*'s wife is not the death of *A*'s widow. When *A* dies without a widow, *A*'s vested remainder in fee tail is inherited by *M* as a present interest in fee tail. *A*'s reversion passes under his will to *P*.

227. *H.   Fee tail.* See problem 226 above.

228. *A.   Present interest* in fee simple absolute. At the time of the conveyance, *A* has a life estate, *B* has a contingent remainder in fee tail, and *O* has a reversion in fee simple absolute. Upon *A*'s death, *X* receives nothing. *B*'s interest is destroyed by the Destructibility of Contingent Remainders Rule because the condition precedent is not satisfied on time.

229. *G.   Possibility of reverter* in fee simple absolute. At the time of the conveyance, *A* has a fee simple determinable. Under the Doctrine of Worthier Title, the interest in the heirs of *O* becomes an interest in *O*. *O*'s will leaves this possibility of reverter to *X*. *S* receives nothing.

230. *A.   Term of years.* *B*'s present interest in a life estate terminates on his death and *O*'s reversion in fee simple absolute becomes a present interest. *A*'s term is inherited by *S* upon *A*'s death.

231. *I.   Fee tail determinable.* *O*'s devise gives *A* a present interest in a life estate, *B* a term of years, and *C* a vested remainder in fee tail determinable. *O* retains a reversion, which includes *O*'s possibility of reverter. *A*'s death terminates *A*'s life estate. *C*'s vested remainder becomes a present interest. *S* inherits *B*'s term when *B* dies.

232. *I. None.* Under the Modified Rule in Wild's Case, *A* receives a present interest in a life estate and the children receive a contingent remainder in fee simple absolute upon *O*'s conveyance. *O* retains a reversion. *O*'s second conveyance to *A* gives *A* a reversion that is a vested interest back to back with *A*'s vested present interest in a life estate. Merger leaves *A* with a present interest in fee simple absolute, merging out the contingent remainder in the children. Upon *A*'s death, *X* receives *A*'s interest by will.

233. *B. Executory interest* in fee simple absolute. *B*'s interest cannot vest until after *A*'s death. Therefore, upon *O*'s conveyance, *A* takes a present interest in a life estate, *O* takes a reversion in fee simple subject to executory limitation, and *B* takes an executory interest. The executory interest remains such after *A*'s death until the condition is satisfied. After *A*'s death, *O* has a present interest in fee simple subject to executory limitation.

234. *L. Fee simple absolute.* At the time of the conveyance, *A*, *X*, and *Y* share a present interest in fee simple subject to executory limitation as tenants in common. The die-without-issue condition is given a definite failure of issue construction. *B* has an executory interest in fee simple absolute. When *X* dies, *S* inherits her one-third undivided share. When *Y* dies, *D* likewise inherits her one-third undivided share. When *A* dies, *T* takes *A*'s interest by will. *A*'s death with issue causes the failure of the condition subsequent, and the executory interest is eliminated. *S*'s share in a fee simple subject to executory limitation becomes a share in fee simple absolute.

235. *A. Present interest* in fee simple absolute. At the time of the conveyance, *A* has a present interest in a life estate, *B* has a contingent remainder in fee tail, *C* has a contingent remainder in a life estate, and *O* has a reversion in fee simple absolute. The two conditions do not involve an age contingency; therefore, there is no preference for vesting. *B* and *C* have alternative contingent remainders that are merged out when *O* conveys his reversion to *A*. *B*'s subsequent marriage is too late.

236. *I. None.* At the time of the conveyance, *A* has a present interest in a life estate subject to condition subsequent, and *O* has a reversion plus a right of reentry. When *O* dies, *H* inherits the reversion and the right of reentry. When *A* fails to maintain the property, *H* does not exercise the right of reentry. When *A* dies, *A*'s life estate terminates naturally, and *H*'s interest becomes a present interest in fee simple absolute.

237. *I. None.* At the time of the conveyance, *A* has a fee tail special (issue to inherit are by his wife, *W*), *B* has a contingent remainder in fee simple absolute, and *O* has a reversion in fee simple absolute. When *W* dies without issue, *A*'s estate becomes a life estate. Then *O* conveys part of his reversion to *A* so that *A* has a reversion in fee tail special (issue to inherit are by his wife, *X*). *A*'s two vested interests (present interest in a life estate and reversion in fee tail special) merge to create a present interest in fee tail special, merging out the contingent remainder in *B*.

(The third exception to the Merger Rule is not applicable here because the fee tail special was created in *A*.) *O* is left with a reversion following *A*'s fee tail special. When *A* dies, his fee tail special descends by inheritance to his son, *Z*.

238.   *A.   Present interest* in a fee tail special. See problem 237 above.

239.   *C.   Reversion* in fee simple absolute. See problem 237 above.

240.   *D.   Life estate pur autre vie* (for the life of *A* or *B*, whoever is the first to die) subject to a term of years in *C*.

241.   *C.   Reversion* in a life estate. *A* stands ready to take if *B* dies first. If *A* dies first, *O*'s reversion will become a present interest.

242.   *N.   Fee simple subject to condition subsequent.* Upon *O*'s death, *A* takes a present interest. *O*'s heirs, *X* and *Y*, receive a right of reentry from *O*. Although the condition subsequent (*A*'s going to jail) occurs thereafter, *A* still has her present interest because *O*'s heirs have not yet exercised their right of reentry.

243.   *H.   Vested remainder subject to open* in fee simple absolute. Upon the conveyance, *A* has a present interest in a life estate, *B*'s children have a contingent remainder in fee simple absolute, and *O* has a reversion in fee simple absolute. When *X* is born, *X* takes a vested remainder subject to open in fee simple absolute, which divests *O*'s reversion. The unborn children then have an executory interest in fee simple absolute. *B* inherits *X*'s interest. If *B* were to have more children, they would share in the vested remainder with *B*.

244.   *F.   Vested remainder* in fee simple absolute. At the time of the conveyance, *A* has a present interest in a life estate, *B* has a vested remainder in fee simple subject to executory limitation, and *C* has an executory interest in fee simple absolute. The condition subsequent (*X*'s death without surviving descendants) occurs and divests *B*'s vested remainder. *C*'s executory interest is transformed into a vested remainder.

245.   *I.   None.* At the time of the conveyance, *A* has a present interest in a life estate, *B* and *C* each have an alternative contingent remainder in fee simple absolute, and *O* has a reversion in fee simple absolute. On *A*'s death, *B* has not yet married. *B*'s condition precedent is not satisfied. *B*'s contingent remainder is destroyed under the Destructibility of Contingent Remainders Rule. *C*'s condition precedent is satisfied. *B* has not married by the time of *A*'s death. *C* takes a present interest in fee simple absolute.

246.   *A.   Present interest* in fee simple absolute. At the time of the conveyance, *A* has a present interest in a life estate, *B* has a vested remainder in fee simple subject to executory limitation, and *C* has an executory interest in fee simple absolute. On *A*'s death, *B*'s vested remainder becomes a present interest. *B*'s marriage ensures that the condition subsequent that would have cut short *B*'s estate will never occur. *C*'s executory interest is destroyed.

247.   *I.   None.* At the time of the conveyance, *A* has a present interest in a fee tail, *B*'s issue (unborn) have a contingent remainder

in fee simple absolute, and *O* has a reversion in fee simple absolute. Upon *X*'s birth, *X* still does not have a vested remainder. *X*'s remainder is contingent on *X*'s survival of *B*. *A*'s death without issue ends the fee tail and leaves *X*'s contingent remainder without support. It is destroyed by the Destructibility of Contingent Remainders Rule. *O* then has a present interest in fee simple absolute.

248. *L. Fee simple absolute.* At the time of the devise, *A* has a present interest in a life estate by devise from *O* and a reversion in fee simple absolute by inheritance from *O*. *B* has a contingent remainder in fee simple absolute. Merger does not occur because of the exception for simultaneous creation. *A*'s conveyance allows merger of *A*'s two vested interests in *X*, merging out *B*'s contingent remainder. *X* has a present interest in fee simple absolute. The subsequent events do not affect this conveyance.

249. *I. None.* See problem 248 above.

250. *L. Fee simple absolute.* At the time of *O*'s conveyance, *A* has a present interest in a life estate determinable, *B*'s heirs (unascertained) have a contingent remainder in fee simple determinable, and *O* has a reversion in fee simple absolute coupled with a possibility of reverter in fee simple absolute. *M*'s going to law school is the condition subsequent on *A*'s estate and *B*'s estate. *A*'s death occurs while the remainder in *B*'s heirs is still contingent (because *B* is not yet dead). *A*'s estate terminates. The remainder is destroyed under the Destructibility of Contingent Remainders Rule. At that time, *O* has a present interest in fee simple absolute. *Y* inherits this interest on *O*'s death.

251. *G. Possibility of reverter* in fee simple absolute. At the time of *O*'s conveyance, *A*, *B*'s heirs, and *O* have the interests and estates designated in problem 250 above. At *B*'s death the contingent remainder in *B*'s heirs becomes a vested remainder in *Z* in fee simple determinable. *O*'s reversion is divested and *O* is left with a possibility of reverter. At *A*'s death, *Z*'s vested remainder becomes a present interest. At *O*'s death, *Y* inherits *O*'s possibility of reverter.

252. *F. Vested remainder* in fee simple absolute. *O*'s conveyance gives *A* a life estate. The unborn children have a contingent remainder in a life estate pur autre vie (for the life of the survivor). The remainder in *A*'s heirs is a remainder in *A* by operation of the Rule in Shelley's Case. Therefore, *A* has both a present interest in a life estate and a vested remainder in fee simple absolute. There is no merger between these two vested interests in *A* despite the fact that the intervening remainder is contingent because of the exception for simultaneous creation. When *A* dies, the contingent remainder in *A*'s children is not destroyed because of the exception to the Destructibility Rule that considers a posthumous child in existence from the time of conception. *M* inherits *A*'s vested remainder. When *X* is born, *X* takes a present interest in a life estate, followed by *M*'s vested remainder.

253. *I.   None.* Upon *O*'s conveyance, *A* has a present interest in a life estate, and *O* (by operation of the Doctrine of Worthier Title) has a reversion in fee simple absolute. *X* buys the reversion, and there is nothing for *H* to inherit on *O*'s death.

254. *A.   Present interest* in fee tail. *O*'s conveyance gives *A* a present interest in a life estate, *B* a contingent remainder in fee tail, *B* an executory interest in fee tail, and *O* a reversion following *A*'s life estate and a reversionary interest following *B*'s executory interest in fee tail. On *A*'s death, *O*'s reversion becomes a present interest in fee simple subject to executory limitation. *B* has an executory interest in fee tail, followed by a reversionary interest in *O* in fee simple absolute. *B*'s contingent remainder is destroyed under the Destructibility Rule. *B*'s marriage gives him a present interest, divesting *O*'s present interest. *B*'s fee tail descends to his son, *T,* on *B*'s death.

255. *H.   Vested remainder subject to open* in fee simple subject to executory limitation. At the time of the conveyance, *A* has a present interest in a life estate, the unborn children have a contingent remainder in fee simple subject to executory limitation, *C* has an executory interest in fee simple absolute, and *O* has a reversion in fee simple absolute. *X*'s interest becomes vested upon birth but remains open to include other children if and when they are born.

256. *O.   Fee simple subject to executory limitation.* See problem 255 above.

257. *N.   Fee simple subject to condition subsequent.* Upon *O*'s conveyance, *A* has a present interest in fee simple subject to condition subsequent, and *O* has a right of reentry in fee simple absolute. *O* has not yet exercised his right of reentry, and *S* inherits *A*'s estate.

258. *P.   None.* At the time of the conveyance, *A* has a present interest in a life estate, *X* has a vested remainder subject to open in fee simple absolute, and *B*'s unborn children have an executory interest in fee simple absolute. When *X* dies, *H* takes *X*'s interest. When *A* dies, *H* (holding the interest of a member of the class of *B*'s children) becomes entitled to distribution at the time designated in the conveyance for distribution. The Rule of Convenience closes the class, and *Y* is excluded. *H* has a present interest in fee simple absolute.

259. *C.   Reversion* in fee simple absolute. Upon *O*'s conveyance, *A* has a present interest in a life estate, *B* has a vested remainder in fee simple subject to executory limitation, *C* has an executory interest in a life estate, *D* has an executory interest in fee tail, and *O* retains a reversionary interest in fee simple absolute. On *O*'s death, *B* takes *O*'s interest. When *B* gets married, *B*'s fee simple is cut short and *C* has a vested remainder in a life estate, *D* has a vested remainder in fee tail, and *B*'s reversionary interest becomes a reversion.

260. *F.   Vested remainder* in fee simple absolute. *O*'s conveyance gives *A* a present interest in a life estate, *B* a vested remainder for life, *C* a contingent remainder for life, and *B* (by operation

of the Rule in Shelley's Case) a vested remainder in fee simple absolute. There is no merger of *B*'s two vested estates despite the intervening contingent remainder because of the exception for simultaneous creation. *B*'s death allows *X* to inherit *B*'s remainder in fee simple absolute. When *C* gets married, *C*'s contingent remainder becomes vested.

261. *I.   None.* Upon *O*'s conveyance, *A* has a present interest in fee tail, *B* has a contingent remainder in fee simple absolute, and *O* has a reversion. The conveyance to *O*'s heirs is the retention of a reversion in *O* under the Doctrine of Worthier Title. *O*'s reversion passes to *J* and *K* under *O*'s will. At no time does *X* take an interest in Blackacre.

262. *F.   Vested remainder* in fee simple absolute. Upon *A*'s death, *A*'s fee tail is inherited by *A*'s issue, *J* and *K*. The two vested interests — present interest in fee tail and reversion in fee simple absolute — in *J* and *K* do not merge because a fee tail does not merge with a fee simple. *B*'s marriage changes *B*'s contingent remainder into a vested remainder that divests the reversion in *J* and *K*.

263. *H.   Fee tail.* *J* shares a present interest in fee tail with *K* as a tenant in common. See problems 261 and 262 above.

264. *E.   Right of reentry* in fee simple determinable. Upon *O*'s conveyance, *A* has a present interest in fee simple determinable, and *O* has a possibility of reverter in fee simple absolute. Upon *A*'s conveyance, *B* has a present interest in fee simple subject to condition subsequent (*A* has a right of reentry) and a determinable (*O* has a possibility of reverter).

265. *M.   Fee simple determinable.* See problem 264 above.

266. *B.   Executory interest* in fee simple absolute. Upon *O*'s conveyance, *A* has a fee simple subject to executory limitation. The condition subsequent (*A* dying without issue) is given a definite failure of issue construction and occurs if *A* has no issue living at her death. *B* has an executory interest in a life estate, *O* has a reversionary interest in fee simple subject to executory limitation, *C* has an executory interest in fee tail, and *D* has an executory interest in fee simple absolute. When *O* makes a second conveyance to *B*, *B*'s executory interest in a life estate merges with the reversionary interest in fee simple subject to executory limitation to produce an executory interest in fee simple subject to executory limitation. (Might the suggested third exception to the Merger Rule be extended to this case?) The birth of *A*'s issue does not change this set of ownerships because it does not satisfy the condition subsequent on *A*'s fee simple estate. *A* may still die without issue living at her death.

267. *F.   Vested remainder* in fee simple absolute. Upon *O*'s conveyance, *A* has a life estate and *B* has a vested remainder in fee simple absolute. *O* has nothing to sell to *X*. The fact that *B* is *O*'s only heir does not bring the Doctrine of Worthier Title into operation.

268. *F.   Vested remainder* in fee simple absolute. Upon *O*'s conveyance, *A* has a present interest in a life estate, *O* has a reversion

in fee simple absolute, *B* has a contingent remainder in fee simple subject to executory limitation, *C* has an executory interest in fee simple absolute. The condition subsequent on *B*'s estate (flunking property) occurs to cut short *B*'s estate. *C* is left with a contingent remainder. *B*'s later marriage satisfies the condition precedent on *C*'s interest. *C*'s interest vests, and *O*'s reversion is divested.

269.   *J.   None of the above is correct.* Upon *O*'s conveyance, *A* has a present interest in a life estate, *B* has a contingent remainder for life, *A* (by the operation of the Rule in Shelley's Case) has a contingent remainder in fee simple absolute, *D* has an alternative contingent remainder in fee simple absolute, and *O* has a reversion in fee simple absolute. When *C* gets married, *D*'s contingent remainder is destroyed by the failure of one of the conditions precedent to *D*'s interest. *B* now has a contingent remainder in a life estate followed by a contingent remainder in *A* in fee simple absolute. The remainders of *B* and *A* are contingent on the same condition precedent. *A* also continues to have her present interest in a life estate. There is no merger.

270.   *F.   Vested remainder* in fee tail. Upon *O*'s conveyance, *A* has a present interest in a life estate and *B* has a term of years to begin on the termination of *A*'s life estate. *C*'s interest follows *A*'s interest under the Piggyback Rule, and *C* has a vested remainder in fee tail subject to executory limitation. *D* has an executory interest in fee simple absolute. *O* has a reversion in fee simple absolute. Upon *C*'s death, *X* inherits *C*'s interest in fee tail but without the condition subsequent because the condition has failed to happen.

271.   *H.   Fee tail.* See problem 270 above.

272.   *D.   Contingent remainder* in fee simple absolute. Upon *O*'s conveyance, *A* has a present interest in a life estate, *O* has a reversion in fee simple subject to executory limitation, *B* has an executory interest in a life estate. *C* has a term of years, *O* has a reversionary interest in fee simple absolute (following *B*'s estate), and *D* has an executory interest in fee simple absolute. Upon the passage of one day from *A*'s death, *B* has a present interest in a life estate, *O* has a reversion in fee simple absolute, *C* has a term of years, and *D* has a contingent remainder to follow *B*'s estate. The condition precedent on *D*'s interest is *D*'s marriage.

273.   *D.   Life estate pur autre vie.* Upon *O*'s conveyance, *A* has a present interest in a life estate pur autre vie, *B* has a contingent remainder in fee tail, and *O* has a reversion in fee simple absolute. The death of *A*'s only child does not change *A*'s estate into a life estate because *A* may have more children.

274.   *D.   Contingent remainder* in fee tail. See problem 273 above.

275.   *G.   Possibility of reverter* in a life estate pur autre vie. Upon *O*'s first conveyance, *A* has a fee simple determinable, and *O* retains a possibility of reverter in fee simple absolute. Upon *O*'s

second conveyance, *B* has a possibility of reverter in a life estate, and *O* has a reversionary interest in fee simple absolute. Upon *B*'s conveyance, *C* has a possibility of reverter in a life estate pur autre vie. The life that determines the length of *C*'s estate is that of *B* or *C*, whichever is shorter. *B* has a reversionary interest in a life estate, and *O* has a reversionary interest in fee simple absolute.

5

The Rule Against Perpetuities

No interest is good unless it must vest, if at all, not later than twenty-one years after some life in being at the creation of the interest.

— *J. Gray*

The Rule Against Perpetuities (RAP) is applied at the time of the conveyance after the interests and estates have been identified. It is not a rule to limit the duration of interests; it is a rule to prevent future interests from vesting too remotely. Let us examine the rule closely.

A. ELEMENTS

1. *Must Vest*

In particular, the rule is used to invalidate contingent remainders and executory interests that vest too remotely. All reversionary interests, present interests *not* subject to open, and vested remainders *not* subject to open are considered vested for purposes of this rule. Contingent remainders become vested when the grantee is born and ascertained and the remainder is not subject to a condition precedent. Executory interests only vest in possession (that is, when they become present interests) or when they are transformed into vested remainders. Present interests subject to open and vested remainders subject to open vest for purposes of this rule when the last member of the class takes a vested interest.

It is the quality of being vested, not merely possessed, that makes the interest valid. Thus, where *O* conveys Blackacre "to *A* for as long as Blackacre is used as a farm," *A* has a present interest in fee simple determinable. *O* has a reversionary interest called a possibility of reverter. Both interests are valid. Even though it may be 500 years before Blackacre ceases to be used as a farm and *O*'s possibility of reverter is transformed into a present interest, *O*'s interest is vested from the time of its creation. On the other hand, where *O* conveys "to *A* for as long as Blackacre is used as a farm, then to *B* and his heirs," the attempted conveyance to *B* is an executory interest. Since executory interests do not vest until they vest in possession, *B*'s executory interest is invalid because it may vest too late. (This problem with the RAP in the second case could have been avoided by creating a possibility of reverter in *O* and then transferring the possibility of reverter to *B*!)

2. If At All

It is not necessary for the future interest to vest. It merely must not be able to vest too remotely, even if the chance of this happening is very unlikely and, in some cases, even medically impossible. The interests of members of a class are dependent on each other. None of the interests must be able to vest too remotely or else all the interests of members in the class are invalid. Thus, vested remainders subject to open may be invalid if an executory interest in a member of the class might vest too remotely.

3. Not Later Than 21 Years

The perpetuities period may be increased by one or more actual periods of gestation but only if the child in each period is born alive. For example, where *O* devises "to my great-grandchildren when my first grandchild reaches 21 and no later," the executory interest in *O*'s great-grandchildren is valid. This is true even though at *O*'s death his wife is pregnant with their first child, *A*, who dies 30 years later leaving his 25-year-old wife pregnant with their first child, *B*, who becomes pregnant with her first child, *C*, when she reaches 21. *O*'s child, *A*, is considered a life in being at the time of the devise, despite the fact that his birth occurs after *O*'s death. *A*'s death is the earliest point at which one may hypothesize that all lives in being at the creation of the interest are dead and, at this point, the 21-year period starts to run. The grandchild, *B*, when she reaches 21, does so more than 21 years after *A*'s death, but the extra time is permitted for an actual period of gestation. The great-grandchild, *C*, is born after the end of the 21-year period, but again the extra time is permitted for an actual period of gestation. Thus *C*'s interest vests in this hypothetical within the 21-year period envisaged by the rule.

Note that the class closing rule (a rule of construction), that a class stays open until it closes naturally if there is no member of the class at the time designated for distribution, is not applicable here because the grantor has manifested an intent to close the class no later than the time the first grandchild reaches 21. Since no great-grandchild may take an interest more than 21 years after the death of a life in being at the creation of the interest (except for periods of actual gestation, which are permitted as shown), the interest in the great-grandchildren is valid under the RAP. Note also that such techniques as artificial insemination, in vitro fertilization, and frozen embryos are not considered under the RAP.

4. *After Some Life in Being at the Creation of the Interest*

The 21-year period is measured from the death of some person who is alive at the time of the conveyance. (The time of conveyance may be delivery of a deed or death of a testator.) Any person alive at the time of the conveyance is included in this designation. The RAP is applied at the time of the conveyance and, if there is any possibility that an interest might vest beyond 21 years after the death of a life in being at that time, it is considered void. Since it is possible that a life in being may die at any time, there must be a way of ensuring that a contingent remainder or executory interest becomes vested within the proper period. Therefore, practically, the rule does not void a future interest if there is a measuring life (or lives) that ensures that the interest will not take beyond the period. In the example given above, *A* is the measuring life. (If measuring lives are specified in the conveyance, they must be reasonable in number.)

For example, where *O* conveys "to *A* and his heirs as long as Blackacre is used as a farm, then to *B* if *X*, *Y*, or *Z* (three healthy children) is alive," *X*, *Y*, or *Z* is a measuring life that ensures that *B*'s interest will not vest too remotely. There is one condition precedent on *B*'s executory interest becoming a present interest: the failure to use Blackacre as a farm during the lifetime of *X*, *Y*, and *Z*. If the condition subsequent were only the failure to use Blackacre as a farm, *B*'s interest could vest beyond the perpetuities period in a holder of *B*'s interest who is not a life in being at the creation of the interest. This possibility would make the executory interest void ab initio and the conveyance valid only as to *A* in fee simple determinable.

Also, where *O* conveys "to *A* for life, then to *B* if *C* gets married," *B* has a valid contingent remainder because *B* or her purchasers or heirs stand ready to take whenever the condition is satisfied and the life estate terminates. *B*'s interest cannot vest beyond the death of *A* because of the Destructibility of Contingent Remainders Rule, and therefore *A* is a measuring life that ensures that the perpetuities period is not exceeded before *B*'s interest vests. Note that *B*'s interest is valid also because it cannot vest beyond the death of *C* (who is therefore a measuring life) since *C* will marry or not within his own lifetime.

On the other hand, where *O* conveys "to *A* and her heirs, but if *A*'s first son (as yet unborn) gets married, to *B*," *B* has no interest. What may be identified as an executory interest in *B* is void under RAP because it may conceivably vest beyond the perpetuities period, whether it in fact does so or not. The following hypothetical demonstrates this possibility: *A*'s son and his future wife may be born after the conveyance. *O*, *A*, *B*, and all lives in being may die, with *A* and *B* leaving sons (heirs) who were unborn at the time of the conveyance. *A*'s son would continue to hold *A*'s present interest in fee simple subject to executory limitation, and *B*'s son would continue to hold *B*'s executory interest in fee simple absolute. Then, 22 years later, *A*'s first son may marry his wife. This would satisfy the condition subsequent beyond the perpetuities period and *B*'s executory interest (now held by *B*'s son) would vest in possession too late. Therefore, the executory interest is void ab initio.

Since the language of condition ("but if") is conditional, the condition is also void and *A* has a fee simple absolute at the time of the conveyance. If the language of condition in this conveyance had been durational, such as "to *A* and her heirs as long as *A*'s first son (as yet unborn) remains unmarried, then to *B*," the executory interest would still have been void, but the durational condition would have remained. *A* would have had a fee simple determinable. This distinction between estates determinable and estates subject to condition subsequent is important for determining what interests remain after the RAP has voided an interest.

It should be apparent from this discussion that the focus of attention when applying the RAP is on the *interest* created in the conveyance and not on the *person* to whom it is conveyed. Once an interest is shown to be incapable of vesting beyond the period of the rule, it does not matter who holds the interest nor for how long thereafter; it is valid. Before an interest is vested, it does not matter that it is held by a life in being if it has the possibility of vesting beyond the perpetuities period; it is invalid.

B.   A SYSTEM TO DETERMINE VALIDITY UNDER RAP[1]

Validity of an interest under the RAP can be determined by asking four questions. If the answer to any of these questions is affirmative, the interest is valid. If not, the interest is most likely invalid and merely needs a hypothetical example of an invalid situation to prove it.

Question 1: Must the vesting events, if they happen, all happen within the period of the rule? A vesting event is an event that must occur before the interest can vest. It may be birth or ascertainment of the interest holder or the occurrence of an event specified in a condition precedent.

Question 2: Must the interest terminate within the period? A life estate measured by a life in being at the time of the conveyance must terminate within the period because the 21 years cannot start to run until the life estate is over.

Question 3: If the Destructibility Rule is in operation within the jurisdiction, does the interest as a contingent remainder, not in a class nor transformable into an executory interest, follow a prior life estate(s) measured by a life or lives in being? Such a contingent remainder is destroyed by the Destructibility of Contingent Remainders Rule if it does not vest on or before the termination of the prior life estate(s). Note that the Destructibility Rule does not apply to equitable contingent remainders.

Question 4: In the case of a class gift, must the class close and the interests of every member of the class vest, if at all, within the period of the rule? Where *O* conveys "to *A* for life, then to the children of *A*'s first-born son who reach age 15" and *A* has no children at the time

---

1. This section is a modified excerpt from my contribution in 3 Thompson on Real Property 494-496 (Thomas ed. 1994).

of the conveyance, the interest in the children of *A*'s first-born son is valid. If no children of *A*'s first-born son are born by the time *A*'s life estate terminates, the children's interest will be destroyed by the Destructibility Rule. If a child is born to *A*'s first-born son, that child (or representative) will become entitled to distribution no later than the death of *A*, thus closing the class on or before the death of all lives in being. No child of *A*'s first-born son would be able to take a vested interest more than 15 years (plus any actual period of gestation) later.

Note that in Question 3 above, the Destructibility Rule will not guarantee validity in the case of a class gift. For example, *O*'s conveyance when *A* has no children "to *A* for life, then to the children of *A* who reach the age of 50" creates an invalid (and therefore no) interest in the children. The hypothetical situation that proves the invalidity of the children's contingent remainder is that the first child of *A* might reach 50 when the second child is 20 (transforming the first child's interest into a vested remainder subject to open and the second child's interest into an executory interest), and then *A* and all lives in being at the time of the conveyance might die at this time and 30 years later the second child might reach 50 causing her interest to vest beyond the period of the rule.

Also the Destructibility Rule will not guarantee validity in the case of a contingent remainder transformable into an executory interest, such as *O*'s conveyance "to *A* for life and then to the first child of *A*, but if that child does not reach 50, then to *B*" when *A* has no children. *B* has an invalid (and therefore no) interest. Without applying the RAP at the time of the conveyance, *B* and the unborn first child of *A* would have had alternative contingent remainders. The hypothetical situation that proves the invalidity of *B*'s interest is that the first child might be born (transforming that child's interest into a vested remainder in fee simple subject to executory limitation and transforming *B*'s interest into an executory interest), then *A*, *B* and all lives in being at the time of the conveyance might die at this time, and then 30 years later the first child of *A* might die causing *B*'s interest (now held by his heirs) to vest beyond the period of the rule.

C. DIGRESSION ON PERSONAL PROPERTY LAW (OR WHY JEE v. AUDLEY SHOULD NOT BE TAUGHT IN THE FIRST YEAR)[2]

Jee v. Audley[3] has been the bane of many a law student's existence. Not only is the case difficult to understand, but it has been widely criticized for the Fertile Octogenarian rule, the indefinite failure of issue construction, the What-Might-Have-Been rule, the construction of the intent of the

---

2. This section is a modified excerpt from Makdisi, The Vesting of Executory Interests, 59 Tul. L. Rev. 366 (1984).

3. 1 Cox 324, 29 Eng. Rep. 1186 (Ch. 1787).

testator, and the all-or-no validity of a class gift.[4] The case even prompted a poetic rendition of its content in "The Sprightly Septuagenarian" authored by a law student in the early '30s.[5]

In Jee v. Audley the testator attempted to convey an executory bequest in personalty. He bequeathed £1,000, the interest to be paid to his wife for life and the principal to go to his niece and the issue of her body, and "in default of such issue" to "the daughters then living" of John and Elizabeth Jee. Sir Lloyd Kenyon, the Master of the Rolls, found that the limitation to the daughters was void for remoteness under the Rule Against Perpetuities. He interpreted the phrase "in default of such issue" as an indefinite failure of issue construction — the condition would be satisfied when the issue of the niece ran out. Since the daughters' interest was contingent on their survival until the niece's line ran out, it was legally possible that the existing daughters would die and presently unborn daughters would be living at the time the niece's issue failed. A violation of RAP existed because the interest of the daughters could conceivably vest more than 21 years after a life in being at the creation of the interest.

The nature of the interests in this conveyance differed from that of interests in real property. *Jee* involved the conveyance of personal property: £1,000. In the law of chattels personal, there was no legal estate in fee tail; the Statute De Donis only authorized a fee tail in land.[6] Therefore, Mary Hall was considered to take an absolute interest in the money with an attempted executory limitation over. Gray maintains that a gift or bequest of the absolute property in a chattel personal can be followed by an executory limitation over — as, for example, in the case of an executory bequest of a painting to *A*, but if *A* dies without issue (with a definite failure of issue construction), then to *B*.[7]

It appears then from an application of these principles governing the law of chattels personal that the niece, Mary Hall, took a present vested absolute interest in the money subject to the use and occupation of the wife for life and subject to being cut short by an executory bequest in favor of the Jees' daughters living at the time Mary Hall's line expired. In such a case, RAP is violated, and the niece receives an indefeasibly vested interest in the money.

The analysis so far is standard fare for this case. Let us move on to Lord Kenyon's dictum in *Jee*: "If [the limitation in the conveyance of the £1,000] had been to 'daughters now living,' or 'who should be living at

---

4. For a discussion of these points, see J. Dukeminier & J. Krier, Property 315-317 (3d ed. 1993); W. Leach & J. Logan, Cases and Text on Future Interests and Estate Planning 687-688 nn. 15-17 (1961); Leach, The Rule Against Perpetuities and Gifts to Classes, 51 Harv. L. Rev. 1329, 1338-1341 (1938). See generally Leach, Perpetuities in a Nutshell, 51 Harv. L. Rev. 638 (1938).

5. See W. Leach & J. Logan, supra note 4, at 689 n. 17.

6. J. Dukeminier & J. Krier, supra note 4, at 316; J. Gray, The Rule Against Perpetuities at 109 (4th ed. 1942).

7. J. Gray, supra note 6, at 741-742, 745. See H. Carey & D. Schuyler, Illinois Law of Future Interests 65 (1941). Butler's Note to 1 Fearne, Contingent Remainders, in W. Leach, Cases and Materials on the Law of Future Interests 217 (1935), confirms that there are no remainders in personal property. The only future interest in a grantee is executory.

the time of my death,' it would have been very good; but as it stands, this limitation may take in after-born daughters."[8]

In 1938, Professor Leach asserted that this dictum was "one hundred per cent wrong."[9] Twenty-three years later, he reiterated the same conclusion in more colorful language:

> Since I consider this case so bad, I take a certain ghoulish pleasure in pointing out that at page 688 Lord Kenyon makes a clear error. He says that if the gift had been to "daughters now living" it would have been good. This is wrong. To make it good the gift would have had to have been to "daughters now living who shall be living at the death without issue of Mary Hall."[10]

In their textbook on property, Professors Dukeminier and Krier concur with Professor Leach's opinion.[11]

If, however, one examines the law of personal property in this area, Lord Kenyon's statement may be taken as technically correct. In Hide v. Parratt,[12] the court of Chancery held that a bequest of personal property to a wife for life and then to a son, Joseph, was valid. It stated that "the rule is, where personal chattels are devised for a limited time, it shall be intended the use of them only, and not the devise of the thing itself, and therefore [the Lord Keeper] allowed the remainder over to be good."[13] Since the wife was considered to have only the use of the personal property, the present absolute interest (subject to the use in the wife) appears to have existed in the son (despite the Court's use of the term "remainder over"). The only other alternative is for the grantor's heirs to have held the present interest subject to an executory interest in the son, but this interpretation is doubtful in light of an earlier 1459 opinion.

The 1459 case[14] permitted the bequest of a Mass book to two people successively for their lives and upon the death of the second person to the parishioners of a certain parish. The case was in trespass, and although its report was inconclusive, it appears that the "life tenants" received a right to the use and occupation of the Mass book while the property or absolute interest remained in others.[15] This case proposes the rule that a gift of personal property is present and absolute in the final grantee subject to the use and occupation of "life tenants."

Relating these precedents to Jee v. Audley, one can formulate an argument justifying Lord Kenyon's dictum. If the bequest had been to Mary

---

8. 1 Cox 324, 326, 29 Eng. Rep. 1186, 1187 (Ch. 1787).

9. Leach, The Rule Against Perpetuities and Gifts to Classes, 51 Harv. L. Rev. 1329, 1341 (1938).

10. W. Leach & J. Logan, Manual for Teachers to Accompany Cases and Text on Future Interests and Estate Planning 171 (1961).

11. J. Dukeminier & J. Krier, supra note 4, at 317.

12. 2 Vern. 331 (1696).

13. Id. at 332.

14. Y.B. Trin. 37 Hen. 6, pl. 11 (1459). For an account of the case, see Paramour v. Yardley, 2 Plowd. 539, 542-543, 75 Eng. Rep. 794, 799-800 (K.B. 1579).

15. See 7 W. Holdsworth, A History of English Law 472-473 (2d ed. 1937); Bordwell, Interests in Chattels Real and Personal, 1 Mo. L. Rev. 119, 129 (1936); J. Gray, The Rule Against Perpetuities 737 (4th ed. 1942).

Hall and her issue and on the indefinite failure of her issue to the daughters now living of the Jees, the daughters now living take a present absolute vested interest subject to the use and occupation of Mary Hall and her issue. Such a present interest is valid under RAP. The use in Mary Hall would be a fee-tail-like interest recognized in an earlier 1565 opinion.[16] The opinion considered a devise of the use of jewels and pieces of plate of the late Chief Justice of England, Lord Fitz-James, to Nicholas Fitz-James and the heirs male of his body. The court held that the grantee of the plate had only the use and occupation.[17]

What has not been recognized by the commentators is that the gift over upon failure of issue with an indefinite failure of issue construction was not necessarily a shifting executory bequest as it was in the actual conveyance in *Jee.* Where the gift over is subject to a condition precedent as in the facts of *Jee,* it is executory; where the "gift over" is not subject to a condition precedent but will take in possession at the end of a life-estate-like or fee-tail-like interest as in the dictum of *Jee,* it is present. Under this reasoning the dictum of Lord Kenyon would be correct.

The bottom line on this digression is that so much criticism, confusion, and consternation devoted to only one case in a first-year Property course justifies its exclusion or at least its postponement to an upper-level course that has the luxury of delving into such refinements.

Problem Set V

The problems in this section ask for a description of an interest or an estate. The answers for interest are:

    A. present interest
    B. executory interest
    C. reversion
    D. contingent remainder
    E. right of reentry
    F. vested remainder
    G. possibility of reverter
    H. vested remainder subject to open
    I. none
    J. none of the above is correct

The answers for estate are:

    A. term of years
    B. term of years determinable
    C. life estate
    D. life estate pur autre vie
    E. life estate determinable

---

16. Owen 33, 74 Eng. Rep. 879 (1565).
17. See 7 W. Holdsworth, supra note 15, at 473 n. 2.

    F.   life estate subject to condition subsequent
    G. life estate subject to executory limitation
    H. fee tail
    I.   fee tail determinable
    J.   fee tail subject to condition subsequent
    K. fee tail subject to executory limitation
    L.   fee simple absolute
    M. fee simple determinable
    N. fee simple subject to condition subsequent
    O. fee simple subject to executory limitation
    P.   none
    Q. none of the above is correct

Problems

O conveys to *A* and his heirs, but if the property ceases to be used for agricultural purposes, to *B* and his heirs.

    276.   What is *A*'s estate?

O conveys to *A* for life, then to *A*'s children (presently unborn) for the life of the survivor, then to their children for the life of their survivor, then to *B* and his heirs. *A*'s first child, *X*, is born two years after *O*'s conveyance. Then *O* dies.

    277.   What is *A*'s unborn children's interest?
    278.   What is *A*'s unborn grandchildren's interest?
    279.   What is *B*'s interest?

O conveys to *A* and his heirs for as long as the property is used as a tavern, then to *B* and her heirs. *O* then conveys all remaining interest that he has in the property to *C* and his heirs.

    280.   What is *A*'s estate?
    281.   What is *C*'s interest?

O conveys to his children who reach 21 and their heirs. *O* has no children at the time of the conveyance. Thirty years later he marries a bride who is 18 years old, and he then dies two months later with his only child in the womb of his wife. The child, *B*, is born ten months later and reaches age 21.

    282.   What is *B*'s estate?

O conveys to the children of *A* who reach 30. *A* is dead at the time of the conveyance and his children are ages 3 and 29.

    283.   What is *A*'s children's interest?

O conveys to the children of *A* who reach 30. *A* is alive at the time of the conveyance and has two children ages 25 and 29.

    284.   What is *A*'s children's interest?

O conveys to the children of *A* who reach 30. *A* is alive at the time of the conveyance and has two children, *X*, aged 25, and *Y*, aged 32.

285.   What is *X*'s interest?

O devises Blackacre to his great-grandchildren when his first grandchild reaches 21. At *O*'s death, *O*'s wife is pregnant with his first and only child, *A*, who is born four months later and dies at the age of 30, leaving his 25-year-old wife pregnant with their only child, *B*, who is born five months later and subsequently, at age 18, bears a son, *C*. *C*'s mother, *B*, reaches 21.

286.   What is *C*'s estate?

O conveys to all his grandchildren who shall be born in the next 30 years. *O* has no grandchildren at this time.

287.   What is the unborn grandchildren's interest?

O devises to all his grandchildren who shall be born in the next 30 years. The grandchildren of *O* are as yet unborn.

288.   What is the unborn grandchildren's interest?

O devises to his great-grandchildren who reach the age of 21 and their heirs. *O*'s children all die before *O*'s death. *O* dies leaving two grandchildren, *A* and *B*.

289.   What is the great-grandchildren's interest?
290.   What is *O*'s heir's interest?

O conveys to *A* (now married) for life, then to *A*'s widow for life, then to *A*'s children then living and their heirs.

291.   What is *A*'s widow's interest?
292.   What is *A*'s children's interest?

O conveys to *A* and his heirs as long as Blackacre is used as a farm. *O* then conveys any interest he has remaining in Blackacre to *B* and his heirs.

293.   What is *A*'s estate?
294.   What is *B*'s interest?

O conveys Blackacre to his wife, *A*, for life, then to his niece, *B*, and the issue of her body, and if she dies without issue, to the daughters of John and Elizabeth Jay. John and Elizabeth Jay are each 90 years old. One year later, *O* dies. Two years later *A* dies, leaving the Jays, their two 50-year-old daughters, and *B* surviving her. *B* does not have children.

295.   What is the interest of the two living daughters?
296.   What is *O*'s heirs' interest?

O conveys to his wife, *A*, for life, then to his niece, *B*, and her heirs, and if she dies without issue, to the then living daughters of John and Elizabeth

Jay. John and Elizabeth Jay are each 90 years old. One year later, *O* dies. Two years later, *A* dies, leaving the Jays, their two 50-year-old daughters and *B* surviving her. *B* does not have children.

297.   What is the interest of the two living daughters?

O conveys to his wife, *A*, for life, then to his niece, *B*, and the issue of her body, and if she dies without issue, to the then living daughters of John and Elizabeth Jay. John and Elizabeth Jay are each 90 years old. One year later, *O* dies. Two years later, *A* dies, leaving the Jays, their two 50-year-old daughters and *B* surviving her. *B* does not have children.

298.   What is the interest of the two living daughters?

O conveys to his wife, *A*, for life, then to his niece, *B*, and her heirs, and if she dies without issue, to the daughters of John and Elizabeth Jay. John and Elizabeth Jay are each 90 years old. One year later, *O* dies. Two years later, *A* dies, leaving the Jays, their two 50-year-old daughters and *B* surviving her. *B* does not have children.

299.   What is the interest of the two living daughters?

O conveys to *A* and his heirs, but if the property is ever used as a bar, to *X* for life.

300.   What is *X*'s interest?

O has one child, *A*, but no grandchildren living at her death. *O* devises Blackacre to her grandchildren.

301.   What is the unborn grandchildren's interest?

O has one child, *A*, but no grandchildren living. *O* conveys Blackacre to his grandchildren.

302.   What is the unborn grandchildren's interest?

O has one child, *A*, and two grandchildren, *X* and *Y*, living. *O* conveys Blackacre to his grandchildren.

303.   What is the interest of *X* and *Y*?

O devises Blackacre to *T* in trust for *A* for life and then in trust for *A*'s children who shall reach the age of 30. At the time of *O*'s death, *A* has one two-year-old child, *X*.

304.   What is *X*'s interest?

O conveys to *A* and his heirs. *A* then conveys to *B* and her heirs as long as the property is used as a farm.

305.   What is *A*'s interest?

O conveys to the children of *A* who are living when the next President of the United States will be elected.

306.   What is the interest of the children of *A*?

O conveys to *A* for life, then, one day later, to the children of *A* who reach 30. *A* is alive at the time of the conveyance and has two children, *M* and *N*, ages 7 and 31 respectively.

307.   What is *N*'s interest?

O conveys to *A* for life, then to the great-grandchildren of *B*. *B* has two children, *X* and *Y*, and one great-grandchild, *Z*.

308.   What is *Z*'s interest?

O conveys to *A* and his heirs as long as the property is used for purposes other than the selling of alcohol, otherwise to *A*'s heirs.

309.   What is *A*'s estate?

O devises Blackacre to *T* in trust for *A* for life, then in trust for *A*'s children who shall reach the age of 25. When *O* dies, *A* is 94 years old and has four living children, *W*, *X*, *Y*, and *Z*, all of whom are over 30.

310.   What is the interest of the four children?

O conveys to *A* for life, then to such and only such of *A*'s children as shall attain the age of 30 and their heirs, then to *C* and his heirs. At the time of the conveyance, *B* is *A*'s only child and is 19 years old.

311.   What is *B*'s interest?

O plans to retire with his wife. His children, with the exception of one who has died, all are grown and making their own way. Some of them have given him grandchildren, but none of the grandchildren has reached 18. *O* then conveys to his wife, *A*, for life, then to his children for the life of their survivor, then to his grandchildren who reach 18 and their heirs.

312.   What is the living grandchildren's interest?

O conveys to *A* and his heirs to have until 21 years and one day after *A*'s death, then to *B* and his heirs.

313.   What is *B*'s interest?

O conveys Blackacre to *A* for 20 years, then to *B* for life, then to the heirs of *B*, but if the land is ever used to sell alcohol as a commercial enterprise, to *C* and his heirs.

314.   What is *B*'s estate?

O conveys to *A*'s grandchildren who shall be living 21 years after the deaths of Alice and Mary.

315.   What is the interest of *A*'s grandchildren?

O devises to his grandchildren. At the time of his death, *O*'s wife is pregnant with their only child, who is born four months later.

    316.   What is the interest of *O*'s grandchildren?

O conveys to *A* for life, then at least one year later to *B*'s grandchildren. *B* has one child, *X*, and no grandchildren at the time of the conveyance.

    317.   What is the interest of *B*'s grandchildren?

O conveys to *A* for life, then at least one year later to *B*'s children. *B* has no children at the time of the conveyance.

    318.   What is the interest of *B*'s children?

O devises to *A* for life, then at least one year later to *O*'s grandchildren who reach 25. *O* has one child, *X*, and no grandchildren at the time of the conveyance.

    319.   What is the interest of *O*'s grandchildren?

O conveys to *A* for life, then at least one year later to *B*'s grandchildren for the life of *B*. *B* has no descendants.

    320.   What is the interest of *B*'s grandchildren?

O conveys to *A* for life, then at least one year later to *B*'s children as long as the land is used as a farm. *B* has no children at the time of the conveyance.

    321.   What is the interest of *B*'s children?

O conveys to *A*'s grandchildren, no matter when they should be born. *A* has two grandchildren, *X* and *Y*.

    322.   What is the interest of *X* and *Y*?

O conveys to *A* for life, then to *B* for life, then, if the old oak tree falls, to *C* and her heirs.

    323.   What is *C*'s interest?

O conveys Blackacre to *A* and *B* as tenants in common. *A* then conveys to *X* until Blackacre is used as a tavern, and then to *Y*. *B* then conveys to *Y* and his heirs. *Y* then conveys to *X* until Blackacre is used as a tavern. These conveyances all take place within the span of one year, and in the following year Blackacre is used as a tavern.

    324.   What is *X*'s interest?

O conveys to *A* for life, then to *A*'s children for the life of their survivor, then to *B* if *B* is then alive, and to *B*'s heirs if *B* is not then alive. *A* has no children.

    325.   What is the interest of *B*'s heirs?

O devises Blackacre to such of *O*'s descendants as shall be living 21 years and two months after the death of *O*. *O* dies leaving two children, *A* and *B*, as his only descendants. *A* has a child, *C*, and then dies five years later, devising all her property to her friend, *X*. *B*, *C*, and *X* are all alive 21 years and two months after the death of *O*.

    326.   What is *B*'s interest?

O conveys to *A* for life, then to *B* and the heirs of her body, then, if *B*'s first son gets married, to *C* and her heirs. *B*'s first son, *X*, is born three years later.

    327.   What is *C*'s interest?

O conveys to *A* for life, then to the grandchildren of *B*. At the time of the conveyance, *B* has one child, *C*, who has no children. Two years later, *C* bears a child, *X*. Then *A* dies. Then two years later, *C* bears another child, *Y*. Then *B* dies. Then *C* bears another child, *Z*.

    328.   What is *Y*'s interest?

In 1995, *O* conveys to *A* for life and then, one day later, to *B* and his issue, then, if *B*'s line of issue runs out before 2031, to *C* until her line of issue runs out.

    329.   What is *C*'s estate?
    330.   What is *B*'s interest?

O conveys to *A* for life, then to *A*'s widow for life, then 25 years after the termination of the life estates in *A* and *A*'s widow, to *B* for life.

    331.   What is *B*'s interest?

O conveys to *A* for 25 years, then to *B* as long as he does not use Blackacre as a farm, otherwise to *C* and the heirs of her body.

    332.   What is *B*'s estate?

O devises to *A* for life, then to *B* and his issue, then to *C* and his heirs if *O*'s first grandchild is a girl.

    333.   What is *C*'s interest?

O conveys to *A* for life, then five years later to *B* and the heirs of his body as long as Blackacre is used as a farm, then to *C* and her heirs.

    334.   What is *B*'s estate?
    335.   What is *C*'s interest?

O conveys to *A* for ten years, then to *B* and his heirs when the University of Tulsa wins their next football game.

    336.   What is *B*'s estate?

O conveys to *A* and the heirs of her body, and if *A* dies without issue, to *B* and his heirs, and if *B* dies without issue, to *C* and her heirs. At the time of the conveyance, *A*, *B*, and *C* each have a grandson, *X*, *Y*, and *Z*, respectively. One year later, *A*, *B*, and *C* each die in a car crash, leaving their grandsons as their only heirs.

    337.   What is *X*'s interest?
    338.   What is *Y*'s interest?
    339.   What is *Z*'s interest?

The day before *B*'s thirtieth birthday, *O* conveys to *A*'s children who reach the age of 30. *A* is impotent and on his deathbed. *B* is *A*'s only child. The next day, *B* reaches 30. Then *A* dies.

    340.   What is *B*'s interest?

O conveys to *A* for life, then to the children of *B* who reach 22 for the life of the survivor, then to the heirs of *A*. *B* has two children, *X* and *Y*, ages 18 and 20 respectively. Three years later *A* dies, leaving *Z* as her only heir.

    341.   What is *Y*'s interest?

O conveys to *A* for life, then to the first child of *A* if that child reaches 25, but if that child does not reach 25, then to *C*. At the time of the conveyance, *A* has never had children. Five years later, *A* has her first child, *X*. Then *C* dies, leaving *Y* as her only heir. Then *O* dies, leaving *Z* as his only heir.

    342.   What is *X*'s estate?
    343.   What is *Z*'s interest?

O conveys to *A* and the heirs of his body, but if *A* dies without issue, then to the children of *B*. *B* dies two years later giving birth to her first child, *X*. One year after *X*'s birth, *A* dies, leaving his son, *H*, as his only heir.

    344.   What is *X*'s interest?

O conveys to *A* and her heirs, but if *A* dies before *B*, then to *B* for life, then to the first child of *B* for life, then to the first grandchild of *B*. At the time of the conveyance, *B* has never had children. Two years later, *B* bears a daughter, *X*. Twenty years later, *X* bears a daughter, *D*.

    345.   What is *D*'s interest?

O conveys to *A* for life, then to the children of *A* for their joint lives, then to the issue of *B* then living for their joint lives, then to *B*'s widow for life, then to *C* and his heirs. At the time of the conveyance, *A* has one child in gestation. *A*'s child, *X*, is born five months later.

    346.   What is *X*'s interest?
    347.   What is *B*'s issue's interest?
    348.   What is *B*'s widow's interest?
    349.   What is *C*'s interest?

O conveys to *A* and the heirs of her body, then to *B* for life, then 22 years after the death of *B*, to *C* if *C* is surviving.

350.   What is *C*'s interest?

O conveys to *A* and the heirs of her body, then to *B* for life, then 22 years after the death of *B*, to *C* if *C* survives the termination of *A*'s interest. One year later, *B* dies. Twenty-five years later, *A* dies without issue. Then *C* conveys her interest to *X* and the heirs of his body.

351.   What is *X*'s estate?

O conveys to *A* for life, then for life to the first child of *A* to graduate from law school, then to *B* and his issue, then to *C* if the first child of *A* to graduate from law school does so before the age of 20.

352.   What is *C*'s interest?

O conveys to *A* for life, then, if *B*'s eldest son gets married, both to *B* for life and then to *C*, but, if *B* has an eldest son who does not get married at any time before that son's death, to *D*. *B* has no children at the time of the conveyance.

353.   What is *C*'s interest?

O devises to *A* for life, then to *O*'s children for the life of the survivor, then to *O*'s grandchildren. At the time of the devise, *O* has one child, *X*, and two grandchildren, *G* and *H*. Three years later, *X* has twins, *I* and *J*. Then *A* dies.

354.   What is *I*'s interest?

O conveys Blackacre to *A* when Blackacre will be used as a farm. One year later, *O* uses Blackacre as a farm. Then *O* conveys any remaining interest in Blackacre to *B*.

355.   What is *B*'s interest?

O conveys to *A* for life, then to *B*'s eldest son for life, but if *B*'s eldest son gets married, to *A*'s heirs. One year later, *B* bears her first son, *Y*. Two years later, *A* dies, leaving *X* as his only heir.

356.   What is *Y*'s estate?

O conveys Blackacre to *A* for life, remainder to *A*'s children and their heirs, but, if *A* has no children alive at the time of her (*A*'s) death, then to *A*'s heirs. *A* has no children at the time of the conveyance. One year later, *A* bears a son, *B*. Then *A* sells all her interest in Blackacre to *X*.

357.   What is *X*'s interest?

O conveys to *A* for life, then to *A*'s first son for life, then one year later to *A*'s first grandson for life, then to *B* and his issue, then to *C* for life. *A* has one son, *S*, whose wife is pregnant with their first son. *B* has never had children.

358. What is the interest of *A*'s first grandson?
359. What is *B*'s interest?
360. What is *C*'s interest?

O conveys to *A* for life, then to *A*'s heirs for the life of the survivor, then to *B* for life, then to *B*'s heirs for the life of the survivor.

361. What is the interest in *A*'s heirs?
362. What is the interest in *B*'s heirs?

O conveys to *A* for life, then to *A*'s heirs for the life of the survivor, then to *B* for life, then to *B*'s children who survive the termination of the preceding estates. At the time of the conveyance, *B* has one child, *X*. *B* dies one year later. Then *A* dies, leaving all interest in the property by will to *X*. *A* has one intestate heir, *H*.

363. What is *X*'s interest?

O conveys to *A* and his issue, and, if *A* dies without issue, then to *B* for as long as *B* is alive, then to *C* if *C* gets married, but, if *C* divorces, then to *D*.

364. What is *D*'s interest?

O devises Blackacre to *A* and his heirs as long as *A* does not have a grandson, then to *B* for life, then to *C*. *O* leaves *L* as his only heir to the rest of his interest in Blackacre. Then *B* dies.

365. What is *A*'s estate?
366. What is *L*'s interest?

O conveys to *A* for life, then to *B*'s children, but, if no child of *B* reaches 25, then to *C*. *B* has no children at the time of the conveyance.

367. What is *C*'s interest?

O conveys to *A* and her issue, then to *B*'s children for the life of *B*, then, if Blackacre is ever used as a farm, both to *C* for life and then to *D*. *B* has no children.

368. What is the estate in *B*'s children?
369. What is *D*'s interest?

O conveys Blackacre to the heirs of *A*'s first child. Two years later, *A* bears her first child, *X*. Then *O* conveys all remaining interest he has in Blackacre to *X*.

370. What is *X*'s estate?

O devises to his grandchildren. *O* has two children, *X* and *Y*, but no grandchildren. Two years later, *X* bears a son, *S*. Then four years later, *Y* bears a daughter, *D*. *O*'s heir is *H*.

371. What is *D*'s estate?

O conveys to *A*'s first son, but, if *A*'s first son dies without issue, then to the now living daughters of *B*. At the time of the conveyance, *B* has two daughters, *X* and *Y*. Two years later, *A* bears her first son, *S*.

  372.   What is *S*'s estate?
  373.   What is *X*'s interest?

O conveys Blackacre to *A* and his heirs. *A* dies leaving *S* as his only heir but devising all his interest in Blackacre to *B*.

  374.   What is *S*'s interest?

O conveys to *A* for life, then to *A*'s children for the life of the survivor, then to *A*'s grandchildren for the life of the survivor, then to *A*'s heirs. *A* has one child, *S*. *S* has one child, *G*.

  375.   What is *G*'s interest?

Answers

  276.   *L.   Fee simple absolute.* The condition subsequent may happen more than 21 years after *A*, *B*, and every other life in being are dead. *A* and *B* may have children, *X* and *Y* respectively. All lives in being may die. *X* and *Y* would take their interests. The property may no longer be used for agricultural purposes more than 21 years later. At that point, *B*'s interest (now held by *Y*) would vest too late. *B*'s interest is void under RAP. *A* has a fee simple absolute since the condition is also eliminated with the invalidation of *B*'s interest.

  277.   *B.   Executory interest* in a life estate pur autre vie. Upon *O*'s conveyance, *A* has a present interest in a life estate, *B* has a vested remainder in fee simple absolute, and *A*'s children have a contingent remainder in a life estate pur autre vie (for the life of the survivor of the children). *A* is a measuring life since *A*'s children must take a vested interest, if at all, within the lifetime of *A*, a life in being at the time of *O*'s conveyance. Upon *X*'s birth, *X* takes a vested remainder subject to open in a life estate pur autre vie, followed by *B*'s vested remainder.

  278.   *I.   None.* What would be the contingent remainder of the grandchildren would vest when they are born. This could happen beyond the perpetuities period since they are not born to lives in being at the time of *O*'s conveyance: *A*'s child, *X*, and *B*'s child, *Y*, could be born after *O*'s conveyance. All lives in being at the time of the conveyance could die. *X* would hold a present interest in a life estate, and *Y* would inherit *B*'s vested remainder in fee simple absolute. The unborn grandchildren would continue to have a contingent remainder in a life estate pur autre vie. Then, more than 21 years later, *A*'s grandchild, *Z*, could be born. At this point, *Z*'s interest would vest too late.

279. *F.   Vested remainder* in fee simple. *B*'s interest vests at the time of the conveyance.

280. *M.   Fee simple determinable. B*'s interest is void under RAP: After *O*'s attempted conveyance of an executory interest to *B* in fee simple absolute, *X* and *Y* could be born to *A* and *B* respectively. Then all lives in being at the time of the conveyance could die, and *X* and *Y* would take *A*'s and *B*'s interests. The property may cease to be used as a tavern more than 21 years later, causing *Y*'s interest to vest too late. Since the language of condition is durational, the condition subsequent is not invalidated, and *O* has a possibility of reverter.

281. *G.   Possibility of reverter* in fee simple absolute. *O*'s possibility of reverter does not change in nature when he conveys it. Note that it is vested from the beginning.

282. *L.   Fee simple absolute. O* is the measuring life to ensure that his children's executory interest vests within the perpetuities period. We may hypothesize that *B*, a child in gestation, may conceivably take beyond an actual 21 years from *O*'s death. His mother may not be a life in being, and when his father dies all lives in being may be dead. Although *B*'s interest might not vest until 21 years and ten months later, the ten months would be an actual period of gestation and, therefore, the interest is valid under RAP.

283. *B.   Executory interest* in fee simple absolute. There will be no more children born; therefore, the children now alive are their own measuring lives.

284. *I.   None. O* attempted to convey an executory interest. It is invalid under RAP: The two living children may die before reaching 30. *A* may have another child and *O* may have a child, and then all lives in being at the time of the conveyance, including *O* and *A*, may die. *O*'s child would inherit her parent's interest. Then *A*'s child would reach 30 more than 21 years later. The last child would take beyond the perpetuities period.

285. *B.   Executory interest* in fee simple absolute. This executory interest is subject to the condition precedent that the child reach 30. Since the older child, *Y*, is entitled to distribution at the time of the conveyance, the class is closed and the only child who has an executory interest is the younger child, *X*, who will take, if at all, within the perpetuities period.

286. *P.   None.* If *O*'s first grandchild reaches 21 before there are any great-grandchildren, there are no members of the class at the time designated for distribution and the class of great-grandchildren remains open until the deaths of all the grandchildren. Since a grandchild who is not a life in being at the time of *O*'s death may have a child more than 21 years after the death of every life in being, that child's interest would vest beyond the perpetuities period. Therefore, the devise to the great-grandchildren is void under RAP. To demonstrate, let us assume that *A* is born, then *A*'s child is born, then *A*, *O*, and all lives in being die, then *A* has a child (*O*'s grandchild) who

reaches 21 before any of *O*'s great-grandchildren are born, and then *O*'s first great-grandchild is born more than 21 years after the death of all lives in being. At this point, the first great-grandchild's interest would vest too late.

Since the Rule of Convenience, which regulates class closings, is only a rule of construction that gives way to a contrary intent in the grantor, a devise by *O*, to his great-grandchildren when his first grandchild reaches 21 *and no later*, would be valid. By this devise *O* would exclude all great-grandchildren born after the designated time. The designated time is no more than 21 years (plus any actual period of gestation) after the death of a child of *O*, and every child of *O* is a life in being. *O*'s child, *A*, born four months after *O*'s death, is considered a life in being. The first grandchild would not be able to reach 21 more than 21 years after the death of this child (except for a gestation period, which is permitted). All great-grandchildren born before this time would have an executory interest in fee simple that would vest in possession at the time the first grandchild reaches 21, which is within the perpetuities period.

287. *I. None. O* might have children; all the lives in being, including, *O*, might die; then *O*'s children might inherit *O*'s present interest in fee simple subject to executory limitation; then *O*'s children who were not alive at the time of the conveyance might give birth to *O*'s grandchildren 22 years later within the 30-year period of the conveyance. The grandchildren's interest would vest beyond the perpetuities period and would therefore be void under RAP.

288. *B. Executory interest* in fee simple absolute. *O* cannot have any more children. He is dead. Therefore, the children are the measuring lives of any grandchildren who are born, that is, a grandchild cannot be born more than 21 years after the death of all lives in being because a grandchild will be born to a life in being.

289. *B. Executory interest* in fee simple absolute. *A* and *B* are the measuring lives since no great-grandchild can be born after they are dead and, therefore, no great-grandchild can reach 21 more than 21 years (plus any actual period of gestation) after the death of all lives in being.

290. *A. Present interest* in fee simple subject to executory limitation to fill the gap before the great-grandchildren take. This interest was inherited from *O* at his death; it was not taken by devise.

291. *D. Contingent remainder* in a life estate. Since *A* may lose or divorce his present wife and remarry, his widow is presently unascertained.

292. *I. None.* This is an example of an "unborn widow." The attempted conveyance of a contingent remainder in fee simple absolute to the children is invalid because, after the conveyance, *A* and *O* may have children and *A*'s widow may be born, then *A* and all lives in being at the creation of the interest may die and *A*'s widow may hold a present interest in a life estate

for 22 years, while *A*'s children continue to hold a contingent remainder (condition precedent is survival) and *O*'s children inherit and hold *O*'s reversion in fee simple absolute, and then *A*'s widow may die and the children's interest would vest after the perpetuities period. Their interest is thus void under RAP.

293. *M. Fee simple determinable.* RAP does not prevent interests from extending indefinitely into the future. It merely prevents them from vesting too remotely.

294. *G. Possibility of reverter* in fee simple absolute. *O* creates a possibility of reverter in himself in the first conveyance and transfers it to *B* in the second. If *O* had attempted to create a future interest (executory interest) in *B* in the same conveyance to *A*, *B*'s interest would have been void under RAP. The possibility of reverter, on the other hand, is always vested for purposes of RAP.

295. *H. Vested remainder subject to open* in fee simple absolute. At the time of the conveyance, *A* has a life estate. *B* has a vested remainder in fee tail. The words "if she dies without issue" are given an indefinite failure of issue construction to complement the fee tail in *B*. Therefore, the daughters of the Jays who are living take a vested remainder subject to open in fee simple absolute. It is subject to open because we may believe (within the confines of RAP) that the Jays may have more children (fertile octogenarian rule). Unborn daughters have an executory interest. The vested remainder subject to open is valid under RAP because the class closes and vests in all its members no later than the death of Elizabeth Jay, who was a life in being at the time of *O*'s conveyance. Taking into consideration the events that have occurred since the time of the conveyance, *B* and the Jays are still alive and, therefore, the daughters still have a vested remainder subject to open.

296. *I. None.* There is no reversionary interest in *O* after he has conveyed a vested remainder (whether it is subject to open or not) in fee simple absolute.

297. *B. Executory interest* in fee simple absolute. At the time of the conveyance, *A* has a present interest in a life estate. *B* has a vested remainder in fee simple subject to executory limitation. The words "if she dies without issue" are given the preferred definite failure of issue construction. The daughters of the Jays have an executory interest subject to two conditions precedent: the death of *B* without issue at that time and the survival of the daughter(s) to that time. Since these conditions cannot be satisfied beyond the death of *B*, who is a life in being at the time of *O*'s conveyance, the executory interest in the daughters is valid under RAP. If both conditions precedent are satisfied, the interest in the daughter(s) will immediately vest (in possession if *A* is dead and as a vested remainder if *A* is alive). The interest in the daughters is not changed by the events subsequent to the conveyance. Upon *A*'s death, *B*'s interest becomes a present interest in fee simple subject to executory limitation.

298. *I. None.* Upon *O*'s conveyance, *A* has a life estate, *B* has a vested remainder in fee tail, and *O* has a reversion in fee simple absolute. The words "if she dies without issue" are given an indefinite failure of issue construction to complement the fee tail in *B*. Therefore, before applying RAP, the daughters of the Jays have a contingent remainder subject to the condition precedent that they be living at the time the fee tail terminates. This interest is invalid under RAP because after the conveyance *B* may have issue, the Jays may have more daughters, and *O* may have a child. Then all the lives in being at the time of the conveyance may die, *B*'s issue may hold the fee tail and *O*'s child may inherit and hold *O*'s reversion for more than 21 years, and then the fee tail may terminate, giving the daughters of the Jays who may then be living a present interest in fee simple absolute too late. Therefore, the interest of the daughters is invalid under RAP.

299. *B. Executory interest* in fee simple absolute. At the time of the conveyance, *A* has a life estate, *B* has a vested remainder in fee simple subject to executory limitation, and the daughters have an executory interest. The words "if she dies without issue" are given the preferred definite failure of issue construction. The daughters of the Jays have an executory interest that must vest, if at all, at the death of *B*. Therefore, the executory interest is valid under RAP.

300. *B. Executory interest* in a life estate. *A* has a fee simple subject to executory limitation. *X*'s executory interest is valid under RAP because it must vest, if at all, in *X*'s lifetime. *X*'s life estate is followed by a reversionary interest in *O*.

301. *B. Executory interest* in fee simple absolute. There are no grandchildren at the time of the devise when the interest is ready for distribution. Therefore, the class of grandchildren will close only on the death of *A*, *O*'s only child. The executory interest of each grandchild is valid under RAP because it must vest in possession, if at all, no later than the death (plus any actual period of gestation) of *A*, a life in being at the creation of the executory interest.

302. *I. None.* The class of grandchildren may include any grandchild born to *O*. *O* may have another child, *B*. Then all lives in being at the time of the conveyance may die and *B* may inherit *O*'s present interest in fee simple subject to executory limitation, and then more than 21 years later *B* may have a child whose interest would vest too late under RAP. Therefore, *O*'s conveyance is invalid.

303. *A. Present interest* in fee simple absolute. The class of grandchildren is closed at the time of the conveyance because *X* and *Y* are born and entitled to distribution. *X* and *Y* take a present interest in fee simple absolute, sharing undivided half interests as tenants in common.

304. *I. None. A* takes an equitable present interest in a life estate and *O*'s heir inherits *O*'s equitable reversion in fee simple ab-

solute. Before applying RAP, *X* has an equitable contingent remainder (conditional on *X* reaching 30). *A*'s unborn children also have this contingent remainder conditional on their being born and reaching 30. *X*'s interest is invalid under RAP because a member of the class of *A*'s children may take a vested interest beyond the perpetuities period: *A* may have another child, *Z*, and *O*'s heir may have a child, *H*. Then all lives in being at the time of the conveyance may die, including *A*, *X*, and *O*. *H* would take the reversion held by *O*'s heir. Since the contingent remainder is equitable, the Destructibility of Contingent Remainders Rule does not apply and *Z*'s interest may transform into an executory interest (still not vested). *Z* may turn 30 more than 21 years later, and his interest would vest after the perpetuities period. Therefore, *A*'s children, including *X*, have nothing.

305. G. *Possibility of reverter* in fee simple absolute. It is prepared to cut short *B*'s fee simple determinable. The possibility of reverter is vested for purposes of RAP. If *O* had conveyed "to *B* and her heirs as long as the property is used as a farm, then to *A* and his heirs," *A*'s executory interest would have been invalid under RAP. The conveyance from *O* to *A* and then from *A* to *B* in this problem avoids such invalidity.

306. I. *None*. Since it is possible, even though very unlikely, that the next President will not be elected until more than 21 years after the death of every life in being at the creation of the interest, the interest is void under RAP: *O* and *A* may have children after *O*'s conveyance, then *O*, *A*, and all lives in being may die and *O*'s child may inherit *O*'s present interest in fee simple subject to executory limitation, and then the next President may be elected more than 21 years later.

307. I. *None*. The attempted conveyance of an executory interest to *A*'s children is invalid under RAP. The older child, *N*, would be capable of taking a present interest subject to open whenever the life estate in *A* terminates and one day passes. Until that time, when he would be entitled to distribution, however, the class of children is open to admit other children born after the conveyance. *A*'s child, *X*, might be born. *N* might have a child. Then *A* might die and the class would close. Then one day after *A*'s death, *N* would take a present interest subject to open, and *M* and *X* would have an executory interest. Then all lives in being at the creation of the interest might die. *N*'s child might inherit *N*'s present interest, and *X* would continue to have an executory interest. Then *X* might live to age 30 at which time his interest would vest beyond the perpetuities period. Therefore, the interest in all the children, including the older child, is void under RAP.

308. H. *Vested remainder subject to open* in a fee simple absolute. Unborn great-grandchildren have an executory interest, but none will receive a vested present interest beyond the death of *A* (except for an actual period of gestation) because the Rule of

Convenience closes the class at the time designated in the conveyance for great-grandchildren to take distribution. This time is at the death of *A*, a life in being, and only great-grandchildren alive at this time (or in gestation and later born alive) will be included in the class and take at this time.

309. *M.   Fee simple determinable.* O attempts to convey an executory interest to *A*'s heirs. The Rule in Shelley's Case does not apply, but RAP does. Following the conveyance, one may hypothesize that *X*, a stranger, and *Y* and *Z*, *A*'s future heirs, may be born. *A* may sell her interest to *X*. Then *A*, *O*, and all lives in being may die. *Y* and *Z* would have an executory interest until alcohol might be sold on the property more than 21 years later. At this point, the executory interest would become a vested present interest too late. Therefore, the executory interest is void, leaving *A* with a fee simple determinable. (The condition subsequent has durational language and therefore remains.)

310. *I.   None.* A has an equitable present interest in a life estate. Before applying RAP, *A*'s born children have an equitable vested remainder subject to open in fee simple absolute since they have already reached 30. Their interest is invalid under RAP because *A* may have another child (remember the Fertile Octogenarian rule) and the heirs of *W*, *X*, *Y*, and *Z* may be born, then all lives in being at the time of the conveyance may die and the heirs of *W*, *X*, *Y*, and *Z* may inherit their estate, then the after-born child's executory interest, contingent on reaching 25, would vest more than 21 years later, beyond the perpetuities period. Therefore, *A*'s children have nothing. *O* has an equitable reversion in fee simple absolute following *A*'s life estate.

311. *I.   None.* Before applying RAP, A has a present interest in a life estate, *A*'s children, including *B*, have a remainder in fee simple absolute contingent on their reaching 30, *C* has an alternative contingent remainder in fee simple absolute, and *O* has a reversion in fee simple absolute. RAP invalidates the interest in *A*'s children because *B* may reach 30 and the interest in *A*'s children who have not reached 30 will transform into an executory interest at that time. *A* and *B* then may have children and die along with all other lives in being at the creation of the interest. *B*'s child would inherit a present interest subject to open in fee simple absolute, and *A*'s child would have an executory interest in fee simple absolute. *A*'s child then would reach 30 more than 21 years later and take a vested interest too late. Therefore, *C*'s interest, which is dependent on the failure of the interest in *A*'s children, is a vested remainder in fee simple absolute following *A*'s life estate.

312. *I.   None.* A has a life estate, the born children have a vested remainder subject to open in a life estate pur autre vie (for the life of the survivor of the children), the unborn children have an executory interest, and *O* has a reversion. The attempted conveyance to the grandchildren is a contingent remainder following the life estate pur autre vie in the children. This interest

is invalid because *O* may have more children (fertile octoge-narian that he is) and *O*'s devisee also may be born; then all lives in being at the time of the conveyance may die, leaving *X* with a present interest in a life estate and *Y* taking *O*'s rever-sion by will; then the children may bear *O*'s grandchildren more than three years later; and then the grandchildren would take a vested interest beyond the perpetuities period. The in-terest in the whole class of grandchildren is void. (If *O* had de-vised rather than conveyed inter vivos, his children would all be lives in being at the time the devise becomes effective (*O*'s death) and the grandchildren's interest would not become vested more than 18 years after the death of every life in being at the creation of the interest. In such a case the grandchil-dren's contingent remainder would have been valid.)

313. *I. None.* Before application of RAP, *A* would have a fee simple subject to executory limitation, and *B* would have an executory interest (which may vest only in possession) in fee simple ab-solute. *B*'s interest is void under RAP because it may vest one day beyond the perpetuities period. One could hypothesize that after *O*'s conveyance the future heirs of *A* and *B* may be born. Then all lives in being might die, and the executory in-terest in *B*'s heir would vest one day too late. Remember that it is *B*'s interest that is void; *B* need not be holding the interest at the time it would vest. Therefore, *A* has a present interest in fee simple determinable, and *O* has a possibility of reverter in fee simple absolute.

314. *L. Fee simple absolute.* RAP voids the interest in *C* and re-moves the accompanying condition. *B* has a present interest in a life estate, and, before application of the Rule in Shelley's Case, *B*'s heirs have a contingent remainder. Under the Rule in Shelley's Case, *B* takes a vested remainder in lieu of the inter-est in the heirs. This vested remainder in fee simple merges with *B*'s life estate to give *B* a present interest in a fee simple absolute subject to a term in *A* (remember the Piggyback Rule).

315. *B. Executory interest* in fee simple absolute. *O* has a present interest in fee simple subject to executory limitation. The inter-est in *A*'s grandchildren is valid under RAP because the sur-vivor of Alice and Mary is the measuring life.

316. *B. Executory interest* in fee simple absolute. The interest is valid under RAP because *O*'s child, being in gestation and later born alive, is considered a life in being at the creation of the interest. The grandchildren cannot take an interest beyond the date of death of this life in being, their parent, except for a period of gestation, which would also be permitted.

317. *I. None. A* receives a present interest in a life estate followed by a reversion in *O*. The attempted creation of an executory in-terest in *B*'s grandchildren is invalid under RAP because *B* may have another child after the conveyance and *O*'s future heir may be born, then all lives in being may die and *O*'s heir would inherit *O*'s reversion as a present interest, and then *B*'s

first grandchild may be born more than 21 years later, causing the present interest in *O*'s heir to be cut short in favor of a vested present interest in the grandchild. This interest would vest too late.

318. *B. Executory interest* in fee simple absolute. *A* receives a present interest in a life estate, followed by a reversion in *O* in fee simple subject to executory limitation. Since vesting on or after one year following *A*'s death is dependent only on the birth of the interest holder to a parent, *B*, who is a life in being, the interest in *B*'s children is valid. Vesting cannot occur more than 21 years after the deaths of *A* and *B*.

319. *I. None. A* receives a present interest in a life estate followed by a reversion in fee simple absolute in *O*. The attempted conveyance of an executory interest to the grandchildren is invalid. Vesting in each grandchild on or after one year following *A*'s death is dependent on the grandchild being born and reaching 25. Although each grandchild would be born to *O*'s child, who is a life in being at the time of *O*'s death, it is possible that the condition (reaching 25) might occur more than 21 years after the death of every life in being. *X* may bear *O*'s grandchild after the conveyance, *O*'s heir also may be born, all lives in being may die, leaving *O*'s heir with a present interest in fee simple subject to executory limitation and *O*'s grandchild with an executory interest in fee simple absolute, and then *O*'s grandchild would reach 25 more than 21 years later. At this point the executory interest in *O*'s grandchild would vest in possession too late.

320. *B. Executory interest* in a life estate pur autre vie. Since the interest will terminate no later than the death of *B*, a life in being, vesting of the interest in any member of the class cannot take place too late. The interest is valid. *O* has a reversion in fee simple subject to executory limitation (following *A*'s life estate) and a reversionary interest (following the life estate pur autre vie in the grandchildren).

321. *B. Executory interest* in fee simple determinable. Since vesting in each child on or after one year following *A*'s death is dependent only on the birth of a child to *B*, who is a life in being, the interest is valid. The condition subsequent on the children's estate has nothing to do with the vesting of their interest. It only determines the length of time during which the estate will last. *O* has a reversion in fee simple subject to executory limitation (following *A*'s life estate) and a possibility of reverter (prepared to cut short the fee simple determinable in the children).

322. *I. None.* The Rule of Convenience, which would ordinarily close the class of grandchildren at the time of the conveyance in this case (because *X* and *Y* are entitled to distribution), does not operate. It is a rule of construction that gives way to the contrary intent expressed by the grantor that all his grandchildren should share in the conveyance. Since a grandchild could be born more than 21 years after the death of all lives in being,

the whole gift is invalid. The attempted conveyance to *X* and *Y* is a present interest subject to open in a fee simple absolute. The unborn grandchildren have an executory interest in fee simple absolute. One could hypothesize that another child of *A* and the heirs of *X* and *Y* may be born, then all lives in being may die, leaving the heirs of *X* and *Y* holding the present interest, and then another grandchild may be born more than 21 years later. This grandchild would take a vested interest too late.

323.   D.   *Contingent remainder* in fee simple absolute. *A* has a present interest in a life estate, *B* has a vested remainder in a life estate, and *O* has a reversion in fee simple absolute. *C*'s interest must vest, if at all, on or before the deaths of *A* and *B*, who are both lives in being. If *C*'s interest has not vested by that time, it is destroyed by the Destructibility of Contingent Remainders Rule.

324.   I.   *None*. *O* conveys a present interest in fee simple absolute to *A* and *B*. *A* conveys her undivided half interest to *X* in fee simple determinable, because the attempted conveyance of an executory interest to *Y* is void under RAP. This leaves a possibility of reverter in an undivided half interest in *A* in fee simple absolute. *B* conveys his undivided half interest to *Y* in fee simple absolute. *Y* conveys his undivided half interest to *X* in fee simple determinable, leaving a possibility of reverter in *Y*. The condition precedent, which is the same for both possibilities of reverter, occurs. *X*'s estate is cut short, and *A* and *Y* are left with undivided half interests as tenants in common in fee simple absolute.

325.   D.   *Contingent remainder* in fee simple absolute. *A* has a present interest in a life estate. *A*'s children have a contingent remainder in a life estate for the life of their survivor. *B* has a contingent remainder in fee simple absolute that must vest, if at all, while *B* is alive (according to the condition precedent). *B*'s heirs have an alternative contingent remainder that must vest, if at all, upon *B*'s death. At that time the heirs will be determined and the condition precedent (*B*'s death before the death of the last child of *A*) will also be determined. None of the interests is invalid under RAP.

326.   A.   *Present interest* in fee simple absolute shared as a one-half undivided interest in a tenancy in common. *O*'s devise is invalid under RAP because the executory interest in *O*'s descendants may vest more than 21 years after the death of all who were alive at the time of the devise. One day after *O*'s death, *B* might conceive a son, *S*, who might be born a month and a half later. (Such facts are considered possible within the confines of RAP.) *S* would have an executory interest subject to open in fee simple absolute. Then within two months of *O*'s death, every life in being at the time of *O*'s death (the time at which the devise is effective) may die. *B*'s son would not take a vested interest until more than 21 years later. At this point, the interest

would vest too late. Therefore, Blackacre does not pass by devise on *O*'s death. It passes by descent to *O*'s children, *A* and *B*. *A* conveys to *X*. *B* and *X* share as tenants in common.

327. *I. None.* *A* has a life estate, *B* has a vested remainder in fee tail, and *O* has a reversion. The attempted conveyance of a contingent remainder in *C* in fee simple absolute is invalid because *B*'s first son and the heirs of *O* and *C* may be born; then all lives in being may die, leaving *B*'s son holding a present interest in fee tail, *O*'s heir holding the reversion, and *C*'s heir holding the contingent remainder; and then *B*'s son may marry more than 21 years later, causing *C*'s interest (held by her heir) to vest too late.

328. *I. None.* The interest created by *O* in *B*'s grandchildren is valid since no grandchild can take a vested interest later than *A*'s death. At the time of the conveyance, *A* has a present interest in a life estate, and *B*'s grandchildren have a contingent remainder in fee simple absolute. Upon *X*'s birth, *X* has a vested remainder subject to open, and *B*'s grandchildren have an executory interest in fee simple absolute. *A*'s death entitles *X* to distribution and the Rule of Convenience closes the class. Only grandchildren who are alive (or in gestation and later born alive) at that time are entitled to take. *X* has a present interest in fee simple absolute.

329. *P. None.* *A* has a present interest in a life estate. *O* has a reversion in fee simple subject to executory limitation. *B* has a springing executory interest in fee tail, followed by a reversionary interest in *O* in fee simple absolute. Before application of RAP, *C* has an executory interest in fee tail. The words "until her line of issue runs out" can be read to create a fee tail. *C*'s interest is invalid under RAP because it could vest too late. One might hypothesize that *B* and *C* may bear issue and *O*'s heir may be born, and then all lives in being may die, leaving *H* to inherit *O*'s interest and *S* to inherit *B*'s interest and *T* to inherit *C*'s interest. One day after *A*'s death, *S* would have a present interest in fee tail, *H* would have a reversion in fee simple absolute, and *T* would have a contingent remainder in fee tail. Then more than 21 years later (but before 2031), *B*'s line of issue may all die, allowing *C*'s interest (now held by *T*) to vest too late.

330. *B. Executory interest* in fee tail. See problem 329 above.

331. *B. Executory interest* in a life estate. *B*'s estate for life ends no later than the death of *B*, a life in being. Therefore, it is valid under RAP. *A* has a present interest in a life estate, *A*'s widow has a contingent remainder in a life estate, *O* has a reversion in fee simple subject to executory limitation and a reversionary interest following *B*'s life estate.

332. *O. Fee simple subject to executory limitation.* *A* has a term of years. *B* has a present interest. *C* has an executory interest in fee tail. *O* has a reversionary interest in fee simple absolute. *C*'s interest is valid because it must vest, if it vests at all, no later than *B*'s death. (*B* can use Blackacre as a farm only during his lifetime.)

333. *D. Contingent remainder* in fee simple absolute. *A* has a present interest in a life estate. *B* has a vested remainder in fee tail. *O* has a reversion in fee simple absolute. *C*'s contingent remainder is valid because *O*'s children are all lives in being. (No child can be born to *O* after his death and this conveyance is a devise.) No grandchild can be born more than 21 years after the deaths of all lives in being since each grandchild is born to a life in being.

334. *K. Fee tail subject to executory limitation.* *A* has a present interest in a life estate. *O* retains a reversion in fee simple subject to executory limitation. *B* has a springing executory interest. *C* has an executory interest that springs (along with *B*'s) from *O*'s fee simple. *C*'s executory interest may also shift from *B*'s fee tail. *C*'s interest is valid because it becomes vested no later than five years after *A*'s death, either as a vested remainder (ready to follow *B*'s present interest in fee tail if it does not cut the fee tail short sooner) or as a present interest (if *B*'s fee tail is over).

335. *B. Executory interest* in fee simple absolute. See problem 334 above.

336. *P. None.* *A* has a term of years. *O* retains a present interest in fee simple absolute. *B*'s executory interest is invalid under RAP because Tulsa may win their next football game more than 21 years after the death of all lives in being. One may hypothesize that the heirs of *A*, *B*, and *O* (*X*, *Y*, and *Z* respectively) may be born after *O*'s conveyance, then all lives in being may die (leaving *X* to inherit the term of years, *Z* to inherit *O*'s present interest in fee simple subject to executory limitation, and *Y* to inherit *B*'s executory interest in fee simple absolute), and then Tulsa may win their next football game more than 21 years later. At this point, *C*'s executory interest (now held by *Y*) would vest as a present interest too late.

337. *A. Present interest* in fee tail. At the time of the conveyance, *A* has a present interest in fee tail, the interest inherited by *X*. The condition "if *A* dies without issue" is given an indefinite failure of issue construction and is superfluous (merely indicating the end of *A*'s fee tail estate). *B* has a vested remainder in fee simple subject to executory limitation. The condition "if *B* dies without issue" is given a definite failure of issue construction. *C* has an executory interest in fee simple absolute. It is valid under RAP because it will become a vested present interest or a vested remainder, if at all, upon *B*'s death.

338. *F. Vested remainder* in fee simple absolute. *Y* inherits *B*'s vested remainder in fee simple. The fee simple is no longer subject to executory limitation because *B* has died with issue, and the condition subsequent to *B*'s estate (condition precedent to *C*'s executory interest) fails.

339. *I. None.* *C*'s executory interest is destroyed by the failure of the condition precedent that *B* dies without issue.

340. *I. None.* RAP invalidates *B*'s interest (the interest of all *A*'s children) because it is an interest of a class, one member of which may take a vested interest too late. One may hypothesize that

B may die before turning 30, A may have another child, O's heir may be born, and then all lives in being may die. At this point, O's heir would inherit O's present interest in fee simple subject to executory limitation, and A's second child would have an executory interest in fee simple absolute. Then A's child may reach the age of 30 more than 21 years later, and the executory interest would vest as a present interest too late. Therefore, O's conveyance is invalid ab initio.

341.   *I. None.* Before application of RAP, O's conveyance gives A a present interest in a life estate, B's children a contingent remainder in a life estate pur autre vie, and A (by operation of the Rule in Shelley's Case) a vested remainder in fee simple absolute. There is no merger between A's two vested interests despite the existence of an intervening contingent remainder because of the exception for simultaneous creation. It is possible for a child of B to take a vested interest beyond the perpetuities period, and therefore the interest in B's children is void under RAP. One might hypothesize that Y reaches age 22 (her interest becoming a vested remainder subject to open, followed by A's vested remainder in fee simple absolute) and she conveys her interest to S, someone born after O's conveyance. B may have another child, M. All lives in being at the time of O's conveyance may die, leaving S with a vested remainder subject to open in a life estate pur autre vie, M with an executory interest in a life estate pur autre vie, and A's heir, R, also born after O's conveyance, with a vested remainder in fee simple absolute. M's executory interest would become a present interest too late (more than 21 years later when M reaches 22). Therefore, O's conveyance creates a life estate in A and a vested remainder in fee simple absolute in A. These interests merge to give A a present interest in fee simple absolute. When A dies, Z takes her interest.

342.   *L. Fee simple absolute.* At the time of the conveyance, the first child of A is unborn. Therefore, before application of RAP, A has a present interest in a life estate, O has a reversion in fee simple absolute. A's first child has a contingent remainder in fee simple subject to executory limitation, and C has an alternative contingent remainder in fee simple absolute. If a child is born to A, that child's interest becomes a vested remainder in fee simple subject to executory limitation, and C's interest (before application of RAP) transforms into an executory interest in fee simple absolute. This classification is due to the Preference for Vesting Exception. The first child of A has a valid interest under RAP because its interest can never vest later than its birth to a life in being. However, C's interest is invalid under RAP because C's heir (Y) and A's first child (X) may be born; then all lives in being may die, leaving A's child with a present interest in fee simple subject to executory limitation and C's heir with an executory interest in fee simple absolute; and then A's first child may live more than 21 years after the

death of every life in being and die before age 25, causing C's interest (now in Y) to vest too late. Since the language of condition ("if that child reaches 25, but if that child does not reach 25") is conditional, the condition is also eliminated. (Remember: words of condition are eliminated; words of duration remain.) A's first child has a contingent remainder in fee simple absolute, and O has a reversion in fee simple absolute following A's present interest in a life estate. When X is born, X takes a vested remainder in fee simple absolute, divesting O's reversion.

343.   G.   *Possibility of reverter* in fee simple absolute. See problem 342 above.

344.   F.   *Vested remainder* in fee simple absolute. Upon O's conveyance, A has a present interest in a fee tail, the children of B have a contingent remainder in fee simple absolute, and O has a reversion in fee simple absolute. The contingent remainder is valid under RAP because it is contingent only on birth to a life in being. The condition "but if A dies without issue" is given an indefinite failure of issue construction and is thus superfluous. When B dies, the class of B's children closes, leaving X with a vested remainder in fee simple absolute. When A dies, his fee tail descends to his son, H.

345.   I.   *None.* Upon O's conveyance, A has a fee simple subject to executory limitation, B has an executory interest in a life estate, O has a reversionary interest in fee simple absolute, and the first child of B has an executory interest in a life estate. The interest of the first grandchild of B is invalid under RAP because it could vest too late. One could hypothesize that B may have a child, X, and O's heir also may be born. X would have an executory interest in a life estate, following B's life estate and followed by O's reversionary interest. B's first grandchild still would have an executory interest. Then all lives in being may die. At this point, X would have a present interest in a life estate, O's heir would take O's reversion, and B's first grandchild would have a contingent remainder in fee simple absolute. Then X may bear B's grandchild more than 21 years later, after the perpetuities period has run.

346.   H.   *Vested remainder subject to open* in a life estate pur autre vie. Upon O's conveyance, A has a present interest in a life estate, C has a vested remainder in fee simple absolute, A's children have a contingent remainder in a life estate and B's widow has a contingent remainder in a life estate. When X is born, his interest vests subject to open in favor of other children who might be born up until the death of A. The unborn children have an executory interest after X's birth. The life that determines the length of X's estate is that of the first child to die, since the estate is for joint lives. X's interest is valid under RAP because the interest of the class must vest, if at all, upon the termination of A's life estate. At that time, the class of A's children closes naturally as well as under the Rule of Convenience.

347. *I. None.* The interest is invalid under RAP. One might hypothesize that, at the time of *O*'s conveyance, it is possible that *X* may not be born alive and thus not considered a member of the class of *A*'s children. *A* may have another child, *B* may have issue, *B*'s future widow may be born, and *C*'s heir may be born. Then all lives in being may die, leaving *A*'s child with a present interest in a life estate, *B*'s widow with a vested remainder in a life estate, and *C*'s heir with a vested remainder in fee simple absolute. *B*'s issue must survive the termination of the life estate in *A*'s children in order to take a vested interest; therefore, they would have a contingent remainder in a life estate pur autre vie. *Y*'s death more than 21 years later would cause the interest in *B*'s issue to vest too late.

348. *D. Contingent remainder* in a life estate. *B*'s widow is unascertained and may even be unborn at the time of *O*'s conveyance. However, *B*'s widow, if any, is ascertained upon *B*'s death, at which time her interest would become vested. *B*'s widow's interest is valid under RAP.

349. *F. Vested remainder* in fee simple absolute. *C*'s interest is vested ab initio and thus valid under RAP.

350. *B. Executory interest* in fee simple absolute. Upon *O*'s conveyance, *A* has a present interest in fee tail, *B* has a vested interest in a life estate, and *O* has a reversion in fee simple subject to executory limitation. The conditions precedent on *C*'s executory interest are the passage of 22 years from the death of *B* and the survival of *C*. The latter condition ensures that *C*'s interest will become vested, if at all, during the life of *C*, a life in being.

351. *P. None.* Upon *O*'s conveyance, *A* has a present interest in fee tail, *B* has a vested remainder in a life estate, and *O* has a reversion in fee simple absolute. Before applying RAP, *O* would have a reversion in fee simple subject to executory limitation, and the conditions precedent on *C*'s executory interest would be (1) the passage of 22 years from the death of *B* and (2) *C*'s survival of the termination of *A*'s fee tail. *C*'s interest is invalid under RAP. We may hypothesize that *O* and *C* may each bear a child, *X* and *Y* respectively. Then *A* may die without issue. Then all lives in being, including *B* and *C*, may die. At this point, *X* would have a present interest in fee simple subject to executory limitation and *Y* would have an executory interest in fee simple absolute. Twenty-two years would pass, and then *C*'s interest (now held by *Y*) would vest too late.

352. *D. Contingent remainder* in fee simple absolute. *A* has a present interest in a life estate. The first child of *A* to graduate from law school is unascertained and therefore has a contingent remainder in a life estate. *B* has a vested remainder in fee tail. *C*'s interest is subject to a condition precedent. This condition precedent must take place, if at all, within 21 years of *A*'s death. Therefore, *C*'s interest is valid under RAP. *O* has a reversion in fee simple absolute.

353. *D. Contingent remainder* in fee simple absolute. *A* has a present interest in a life estate. *B* has a contingent remainder in a life estate. The interests of *B* and *C* are both contingent on *B's* eldest son being born and getting married. *B's* contingent remainder must vest, if at all, on or before the termination of *A's* life estate or it will never vest. The Destructibility of Contingent Remainders Rule destroys any contingent remainder that has failed to vest on or before the termination of the preceding estates. Likewise, *C's* interest must vest, if at all, on or before the termination of *A's* and *B's* estates. Since *A's* estate and *B's* estate can terminate only on or before their deaths and they are lives in being, *B's* and *C's* interests are valid under RAP. *D* has an alternative contingent remainder that is contingent on *B's* having an eldest son who does not get married before his death. This condition must be satisfied, if at all, on or before the termination of *A's* life estate, or *D's* remainder will be destroyed by the Destructibility of Contingent Remainders Rule. Vesting means that *B* must have an eldest son and that eldest son must die without getting married before *A's* life estate terminates. Because of the Backup Rule, *O* has a reversion in fee simple absolute.

354. *H. Vested remainder subject to open* in fee simple absolute shared as a tenancy in common with the other grandchildren. At the time of the conveyance, *A* has a present interest in a life estate, *X* has a vested remainder in a life estate, and the unborn grandchildren have an executory interest in fee simple absolute until they are born. At birth, the vested remainder in fee simple absolute in the living grandchildren opens to receive them. The class closes so as to eliminate this executory interest when *X* dies (natural closing) or when *A's* life estate and *X's* life estate both terminate (time for distribution designated by the Rule of Convenience). Therefore, no grandchild in the class may take a vested interest after the death of all lives in being, and the vested remainder in the living grandchildren is valid under RAP. When *A* dies, *X* has a present interest in a life estate; *G, H, I,* and *J* have a vested remainder subject to open in fee simple absolute; and the unborn grandchildren have an executory interest in fee simple absolute.

355. *A. Present interest* in fee simple absolute. *O's* attempted conveyance of an executory interest to *A* is invalid under RAP because Blackacre may be used as a farm more than 21 years after the death of every life in being at the creation of the interest. One may hypothesize that, after *O's* conveyance, *O's* future heir, *X,* is born and *A's* future heir, *Y,* is born. Then all lives in being may die, leaving *X* with *O's* present interest and *Y* with *A's* executory interest. Then Blackacre may be used as a farm more than 21 years later. At this point, *A's* interest (now held by *Y*) would vest too late. Therefore, *O's* second conveyance to *B* is the entire present interest in fee simple absolute.

356.   *C.   Life estate.* Upon *O*'s conveyance, *A* has a present interest in a life estate, *B*'s eldest son, who is unborn, has a contingent remainder for life, and *O* has a reversion in fee simple absolute. The attempted creation of an executory interest in *A*'s heirs (prepared to cut short a life estate subject to executory limitation in *B*'s eldest son) is invalid under RAP. To demonstrate this invalidity, one might hypothesize that *B*'s son, *Y*, and *A*'s future heir, *H*, and *O*'s future heir, *P*, may be born (*Y* taking a vested remainder in a life estate subject to executory limitation); all lives in being may die, leaving *Y* with a present interest in a life estate subject to executory limitation, *H* with an executory interest, and *P* with the reversion; and then *B*'s son would marry more than 21 years later, allowing *A*'s heir to take a vested present interest beyond the perpetuities period. Therefore, when *Y* is born, his interest becomes a vested remainder in a life estate, and, when *A* dies, it becomes a present interest in a life estate, followed by a reversion in fee simple absolute in *O*.

357.   *J.   None of the above is correct.* Upon *O*'s conveyance, *A* has a present interest in a life estate, *O* has a reversion in fee simple absolute, and *A*'s children (yet unborn) have a contingent remainder in fee simple subject to executory limitation. *A*'s heirs would have a contingent remainder (subject to the conditions precedent of ascertainment and the failure of *A* to bear children by her death) in fee simple absolute, but the Rule in Shelley's Case transforms this remainder in the heirs into a remainder in *A*. Therefore, *A* has a contingent remainder (subject to the condition precedent of failure to bear children by his death) in fee simple absolute. These interests are all valid under RAP because the interest in the unborn children vests in each upon birth (to a life in being), and *A*'s contingent remainder vests when *A* (a life in being) dies without children alive at her death. When *A* bears a child, *B*, that child takes a vested remainder subject to open in fee simple subject to executory limitation. *A*'s contingent remainder transforms into an executory interest that stands ready to cut short the interest in *B* if *A* has no children alive at the time of his death. *A*'s unborn children have an executory interest in fee simple absolute. When *A* sells her interest in Blackacre to *X*, *X* has a present interest in a life estate and an executory interest in fee simple absolute.

358.   *I.   None.* Before application of RAP, *A* has a present interest in a life estate, *S* has a vested remainder in a life estate, *O* has a reversion in fee simple, *A*'s first grandson has an executory interest (conditions precedent are birth and passage of one year from termination of preceding estates) in a life estate, *B* has an executory interest in fee tail, *C* has an executory interest in a life estate, and *O* has a reversionary interest in fee simple absolute. The interest of *A*'s first grandson is invalid under RAP. One may hypothesize that *S*'s first son may never be born. *A* may have another child, *T*. *O*'s future heir, *H*, and *B*'s issue, *I*,

may be born. All lives in being may die, leaving *H* with a present interest subject to executory limitation, *A*'s first grandson with an executory interest in a life estate, *I* with an executory interest in fee tail, and *H* with a reversionary interest in fee simple absolute. Then more than 21 years later *T* may bear *A*'s first grandson, *X*, and *X* would take a vested present interest too late.

359.   B.   *Executory interest* in fee tail. Since the interest in *A*'s first grandson is void under RAP (see problem 358 above), *A* has a present interest in a life estate, *S* has a vested remainder in a life estate, *O* has a reversion in fee simple subject to executory limitation, *B* has an executory interest (condition precedent is passage of one year from termination of preceding estates) in fee tail, *C* has an executory interest in a life estate, and *O* has a reversionary interest in fee simple absolute. *B*'s interest is valid because it vests, if at all, no later than one year after the termination of the preceding life estates in *A* and *S*, who are both lives in being.

360.   B.   *Executory interest* in a life estate. See problem 359 above. *C*'s interest is valid because it vests, if at all, no later than one year after the termination of the life estates in *A* and *S*, who are both lives in being. Also, *C*'s interest is valid because it must vest, if at all, while *C*, a life in being, is alive. When *C* dies, *C*'s life estate is over.

361.   D.   *Contingent remainder* in a life estate pur autre vie. *A* has a present interest in a life estate. *B* has a vested remainder in a life estate, and *O* has a reversion in fee simple absolute. *A*'s heirs and *B*'s heirs each have contingent remainders. The Rule in Shelley's Case does not apply when the estate of the heirs is a life estate. *A*'s heirs are determined at the time of *A*'s death, at which time they take a vested present interest (assuming that there are heirs and that *A*'s life estate has not terminated before *A*'s death). Therefore, the interest in *A*'s heirs is valid under RAP because it must vest, if at all, upon the death of a life in being.

362.   D.   *Contingent remainder* in a life estate pur autre vie. *B*'s heirs are determined at the time of *B*'s death, at which time they take either a present interest or a vested remainder (assuming that there are heirs and that the preceding life estates have not terminated before *B*'s death). Therefore, their interest is valid under RAP.

363.   I.   *None.* *X*'s interest is void under RAP. Upon *O*'s conveyance, *A* has a present interest in a life estate, *A*'s heirs have a contingent remainder in a life estate pur autre vie, *B* has a vested remainder in a life estate, and *O* has a reversion in fee simple absolute. Upon *A*'s death, *H* takes a present interest in a life estate and *O* has a reversion in fee simple absolute. Before application of RAP, *B*'s children would have had a contingent remainder in fee simple absolute upon *O*'s conveyance. One might hypothesize that *A*'s future heir, *F*, and *B*'s child, *G*, and

O's future heir, *J*, then may be born; all lives in being may die, leaving *F* with a present interest in a life estate, *J* with the reversion in fee simple absolute, and *G* with the contingent remainder in fee simple absolute; then *F* may die more than 21 years later, giving *G* a vested present interest too late. Therefore, the interest in *B*'s children is invalid ab initio.

364. *B.* *Executory interest* in fee simple absolute. *A* has a present interest in fee tail. The condition "if *A* dies without issue" is superfluous because it is given an indefinite failure of issue construction (following a fee tail estate). Therefore, *B* has a vested remainder. *B*'s estate is a life estate because the words "for as long as *B* is alive" define the limits of a life estate. *C* has a contingent remainder in fee simple subject to executory limitation. The condition precedent on *C*'s interest is *C*'s marriage. The condition subsequent on *C*'s estate is *C*'s divorce. *O* has a reversion in fee simple absolute.

365. *M.* *Fee simple determinable.* Upon *O*'s conveyance, *A* has a present interest in fee simple subject to executory limitation, *B* has an executory interest in a life estate, and *L* has a reversionary interest in fee simple absolute. *B*'s interest is valid under RAP because it must vest before *B*, a life in being, dies (or else *B*'s interest is over). When *B* dies, *A* is left with a present interest in fee simple determinable, and *L* has a possibility of reverter in fee simple absolute. The attempted conveyance of an executory interest in fee simple absolute to *C* is invalid under RAP because one might hypothesize that *A*'s child and heir, *X*, and *C*'s heir, *H*, may be born; then all lives in being may die, leaving *X* with the present interest in fee simple subject to executory limitation and *H* with *C*'s executory interest in fee simple absolute; then *X* may have *A*'s first grandson, *G*, more than 21 years later, allowing *C*'s heir, *H*, to take a vested interest too late.

366. *G.* *Possibility of reverter* in fee simple absolute. See problem 365 above.

367. *I.* *None.* *B*'s children are unborn. Before application of RAP, their interest would be a contingent remainder in fee simple subject to executory limitation. *C* would have an alternative contingent remainder in fee simple absolute that would stand ready to take whenever *A*'s life estate terminated subject to the condition precedent that no child of *B* be born. If *B* were to bear a child, that child would have a vested remainder subject to open (for future-born children) in a fee simple subject to executory limitation. *B*'s unborn children would have an executory interest in fee simple absolute. *C*'s remainder would transform into an executory interest subject to the condition precedent that *B* and all his children die without any child of *B* reaching 25. *C*'s interest is invalid under RAP because one might then hypothesize that *C*'s future heir, *H*, may be born; then all lives in being may die, leaving *X* with a present interest in fee simple subject to executory limitation, and *H* with an

executory interest in fee simple absolute; and then *X* may die before reaching 25 but more than 21 years later, at which time *H*, holding *C*'s interest, would take a vested interest too late. Therefore, at the time of *O*'s conveyance, *A* has a present interest in a life estate, *O* has a reversion in fee simple absolute, and *B*'s children have a contingent remainder in fee simple absolute. The condition subsequent on the interest of *B*'s children uses conditional language and is considered void along with *C*'s interest. (Note that before application of RAP, *C*'s interest is a contingent remainder that may take upon the termination of the preceding life estate in *A*, a life in being, but the Destructibility of Contingent Remainders Rule does not ensure that *C*'s interest is valid upon application of RAP. *C*'s interest may transform into an executory interest here, and it is invalid under RAP because it may vest not merely upon the termination of the preceding life estate but also by cutting short an estate in fee simple beyond the perpetuities period.

368. *D.   Life estate pur autre vie.* Upon *O*'s conveyance, *A* has a present interest in fee tail, *B*'s children have a contingent remainder in a life estate measured by the life of *B*, *C* has a contingent remainder in a life estate, and *O* has a reversion in fee simple absolute. The remainder in *B*'s children is contingent on birth to *B*, a life in being, and is therefore valid under RAP.

369. *I.   None. O*'s conveyance gives a contingent remainder to *C* in a life estate. The remainder is contingent on Blackacre's use as a farm, a condition precedent that may occur more than 21 years after the death of every life in being. *C*'s interest is valid because it cannot vest after *C*'s death since it is measured by *C*'s life. The attempted conveyance of a contingent remainder in fee simple absolute to *D*, however, is invalid under RAP. One may hypothesize that *A*'s issue (*I*), *O*'s future heir (*S*), and *D*'s heir (*H*), may be born after *O*'s conveyance; then all lives in being may die, leaving *I* with a present interest in fee tail, *S* with *O*'s reversion, and *H* with *D*'s contingent remainder; and then Blackacre may be used as a farm more than 21 years later so as to vest *H*'s interest as a vested remainder too late.

370. *L.   Fee simple absolute. O*'s first attempted conveyance of an executory interest in fee simple absolute to the heirs of *A*'s first child is invalid under RAP. One may hypothesize that *A*'s first child, *X*, and *O*'s heir, *H*, and *X*'s future heir, *T*, may be born; then all lives in being may die, leaving *H* with *O*'s present interest in fee simple subject to executory limitation; and then *A*'s first child may live for more than 21 years after the death of all lives in being and then die, leaving *T* to take a vested present estate too late. Therefore, *O* has a present interest in fee simple absolute after his first invalid conveyance. He conveys this interest to *X*.

371. *L.   Fee simple absolute.* The devise to the grandchildren is valid under RAP. The grandchildren have an executory interest in fee simple absolute until they are born, at which time they take

a present interest subject to open in a fee simple absolute. The interest of each grandchild vests no later than birth to a life in being, *X* or *Y*, because there can be no more children born to *O*, who is dead. The class closes with the death of *X* and *Y*.

372. *L.   Fee simple absolute.* At the time of *O*'s conveyance, *A*'s first son (being unascertained) has an executory interest. Before application of RAP, the estate of *A*'s first son would be a fee simple subject to executory limitation. The condition subsequent would be the death of *A*'s first son without issue living at his death (definite failure of issue construction). *X* and *Y* would share as tenants in common in an executory interest in fee simple absolute. This executory interest is invalid under RAP. One might hypothesize that *A*'s son, *G*, and the heirs of *X* and *Y* may be born; all lives in being may die, leaving *G* with *O*'s present interest in fee simple subject to executory limitation, and the heirs of *X* and *Y* with their executory interest in fee simple absolute; and then *G* may live for more than 21 years and die without issue, allowing the interest of the heirs of *X* and *Y* to vest too late. Since the interest of *X* and *Y* is invalid, and the condition subsequent on the estate of *A*'s first son ("but if *A*'s first son dies without issue") uses conditional language, the condition subsequent is also invalid. *O*'s conveyance gives *A*'s first son an executory interest in fee simple absolute, which becomes a present interest in *S* upon *S*'s birth.

373. *I.   None.* See problem 372 above.

374. *I.   None.* *O*'s conveyance gives *A* a present interest in fee simple absolute. Upon *A*'s death, *B* takes this interest by will. *S* never receives anything.

375. *I.   None.* Upon *O*'s conveyance, *A* has a present interest in a life estate, *S* has a vested remainder subject to open in a life estate pur autre vie, and the unborn children have an executory interest in a life estate pur autre vie. The interest in *A*'s heirs is an interest in *A* under the Rule in Shelley's Case. Therefore, *A* also has a vested remainder in fee simple absolute. The interest in *A*'s grandchildren (including *G*) is invalid under RAP. Before application of RAP, *G* would have had a vested remainder subject to open in a life estate pur autre vie (following *S*'s life estate pur autre vie and followed by *A*'s vested remainder), and *A*'s unborn grandchildren would have had an executory interest in a life estate pur autre vie. One might hypothesize that *A* may have another child, *T*, and *G*'s future heir, *R*, may be born; then all lives in being may die, leaving *T* with a present interest in a life estate, *R* with a vested remainder subject to open in a life estate pur autre vie, *T* with a vested remainder in fee simple absolute, and *A*'s unborn grandchildren with an executory interest in a life estate pur autre vie; and then *T* may have a child, *Z*, more than 21 years later, allowing *Z* to take a vested interest too late under RAP.

6

Powers of Appointment

A. DEFINITIONS

It is possible for a donor to give a power to a donee to create a future interest in the donor's property. For example, *O* may convey a life estate to *A* and give *A* a power to appoint the rest of the property to one of *A*'s children, otherwise the remainder in fee simple absolute after the life estate to go to *B*. *O* is the *donor* of the power to sell; *A* is the *donee*; *A*'s children are the *objects of the power*; the child who actually receives the property is the *appointee*; and *B* is the *taker in default of appointment* of the gift over in default of appointment.

The appointee generally is considered a taker from the donor, not from the donee, and the exercise of the power of appointment is said generally to relate back to the creation of the power (the relation back doctrine). However, the appointment may not be made by the donee to one who has died before the appointment even though the death of the appointee be after the power has been created by the donor.

If there are no contingencies on the interest of the taker of the gift over in default of appointment, it is considered vested at the time of its creation subject to divestment by the exercise of the power of appointment. Exercise of a power involves exercise of a condition subsequent cutting short the gift over in default of appointment. Thus, in a conveyance "to *A* for life with power in *A* to dispose of the remainder in fee simple absolute after the life estate; otherwise to *B*," the remainder to *B* in default of appointment is vested in fee simple subject to executory limitation. It is possible for the gift over in default of appointment to be contingent by its terms, such as in the conveyance "to *A* for life with power in *A* to dispose of the remainder in fee simple absolute after the life estate; otherwise to *B* if B *gets married*." However, the nonexercise of the power itself is not a condition precedent; the exercise of the power is a condition subsequent.

B. TYPES OF POWERS

There are six types of powers:

(A) A *general power of appointment* can be exercised in favor of anyone, including the donee. It may be
(1) testamentary or exercisable by will,
(2) exercisable by deed, or
(3) exercisable by deed or will.
(B) A *special power of appointment* can be exercised only in favor of a group of persons not including the donee or his estate, creditors, or creditors of his estate. It may be
(1) testamentary or exercisable by will,
(2) exercisable by deed, or
(3) exercisable by deed or will.

Furthermore, the special power may be *exclusive* or *nonexclusive*. If each member of the group must receive some minimum amount by the appointment, it is nonexclusive. Otherwise, it is exclusive; the donee may or may not appoint to every member of the group.

C. RULES

A donee of a general power may exercise his power as if he were disposing of his own property. If the power is not exercised or is exercised only partially, the property not appointed passes to the takers in default of appointment or, if there are none, back to the donor who holds the reversion.

A donee of a special power is restricted by the limitations imposed by the donor. If the power is not exercised, the property not appointed passes to the takers in default of appointment designated in the conveyance or, if there are no express takers in default of appointment, then to the class of appointees in equal parts. The class of appointees are considered implied takers in default of appointment. If the appointment under a nonexclusive power excludes a member of the group it is completely invalid and passes to the takers in default of appointment, either express or implied. If the appointment under a special power otherwise violates the restrictions imposed by the donor, only that part of the appointment that does not violate the restrictions is valid; the other part passes to the takers in default, express or implied. If there is no restriction placed by the donor against a partial exercise of the special power, such an exercise is valid.

A power of appointment, general or special, is personal to the donee and cannot be transferred or assigned, but a further power of appointment may be created during the exercise of a power. *A power of appoint-*

ment may be released, unless it is a power in one who has no interest in the property and it is to be exercised for the benefit of another.

To *create* a power of appointment, no special words are necessary as long as the donor manifests an intent to do so implicitly or explicitly. Care must be taken to avoid precatory words. To *exercise* a power of appointment, no special words are necessary as long as the intent to exercise is shown, except in the case of a will. In a will there generally must be reference to the subject of the power or to the power itself, unless it be in a case where the will would be inoperative without the aid of the power and the intention to execute the power was clear and manifest. Courts have permitted the exercise of a general or a special power in a will without specific reference to the power, such as in the general residuary clause of a will, but this is a minority position and contrary to the Uniform Probate Code.

D.   RULE AGAINST PERPETUITIES

The Rule Against Perpetuities applies to powers of appointment in three respects:

(1)   the validity of the power,
(2)   the validity of the appointed interests, and
(3)   the validity of the interest in default of appointment.

The *validity of the power* is determined for:

(A)   special powers and general testamentary powers by whether it is possible for the power *to be exercised* beyond the perpetuities period as measured from the time the power is created, and

(B)   general powers exercisable by deed or by deed or will by whether it is possible for the power *to be acquired* beyond the perpetuities period as measured from the time the power is created.

The *validity of the appointed interests* is determined for:

(A)   special powers and general testamentary powers by applying the RAP at the time the *power is created* as if the appointed interests are created in the instrument creating the power, but taking into consideration the facts existing at the time the appointment is made (sometimes referred to as the "second look" doctrine), and

(B)   general powers exercisable by deed or by deed or will by applying the RAP at the time the *appointed interests are created* (the relation back doctrine mentioned at the beginning of this chapter is not applicable in this case).

The *validity of the interest in default of appointment* is determined for:

(A)   powers that are invalid under the RAP by applying the RAP as if the interest is an ordinary interest and not a gift in default of appointment, and

(B)   powers that are valid under the RAP by applying the RAP as if, at the moment the power expires (by death of the donee, release or otherwise), the donee makes an appointment in the exact terms of the gift in default of appointment.

Problem Set VI

The problems in this section ask for a description of an interest, an estate, or a power of appointment. The answers for interest are:

A.   present interest
B.   executory interest
C.   reversion
D.   contingent remainder
E.   right of reentry
F.   vested remainder
G.   possibility of reverter
H.   vested remainder subject to open
I.   none
J.   none of the above is correct

The answers for estate are:

A.   term of years
B.   term of years determinable
C.   life estate
D.   life estate pur autre vie
E.   life estate determinable
F.   life estate subject to condition subsequent
G.   life estate subject to executory limitation
H.   fee tail
I.   fee tail determinable
J.   fee tail subject to condition subsequent
K.   fee tail subject to executory limitation
L.   fee simple absolute
M.   fee simple determinable
N.   fee simple subject to condition subsequent
O.   fee simple subject to executory limitation
P.   none
Q.   none of the above is correct

The answers for power of appointment are:

A.   valid general testamentary power of appointment
B.   valid general power of appointment exercisable by deed

C.   valid general power of appointment exercisable by deed or will
D.   valid special testamentary power of appointment
E.   valid special power of appointment exercisable by deed
F.   valid special power of appointment exercisable by deed or will
G.   invalid general testamentary power of appointment
H.   invalid general power of appointment exercisable by deed
I.   invalid general power of appointment exercisable by deed or will
J.   invalid special testamentary power of appointment
K.   invalid special power of appointment exercisable by deed
L.   invalid special power of appointment exercisable by deed or will

Problems

O conveys to A with the power to use the property as she sees fit.

376.   What is A's estate?

O conveys to A for life with the power to give the property by will as she sees fit, but failing such disposition, upon her death to X. X is A's only living child at the time of the conveyance.

377.   What is A's estate?

O conveys to A for life, then to such of his children as he may by will appoint, and in default of appointment, to C.

378.   What is C's interest?

O conveys to A for life, then to A's oldest child for life, then to X, Y, or Z as A's oldest child shall appoint during their lives, and in default of appointment to S and her heirs. A's oldest child, B, is born two years later and when she reaches majority at 18, she appoints to X and his heirs.

379.   At the time of conveyance, what is the power of appointment of A's oldest child?
380.   What is X's interest now?

O conveys to A for life, then to A's grandchildren for their joint lives, then to whomever the first grandchild of A shall appoint. Three years later A has his first grandchild, M. Seventeen years later M has his first child, X, to whom he appoints the estate.

381.   At the time of conveyance, what is the power of appointment of A's first grandchild?
382.   What is X's interest now?

O conveys to A for life, then to A's oldest child for life, then to whomever A's oldest child shall appoint. A's oldest child, X, is born two years later and when she reaches the age of 25, she appoints to the children of B and their heirs. *B* is one year old at the time of the exercise of the appointment.

383.   At the time of conveyance, what is the power of appointment of *A*'s oldest child?
384.   What is *B*'s children's interest now?

O devises to his wife, *A*, for life, then, one year later, to whomever *A* shall appoint, and in default of appointment, to *A*'s grandchildren when they reach 30 years of age. *A* fails to appoint and at her death (six years after *O*'s conveyance) her children are all dead, although she does have a one and only grandchild, age three.

385.   What is the interest of the grandchild?

O conveys to *A* for life, then to such of *A*'s issue as *A* shall appoint, and in default of appointment to *S*. *A*'s child, *B*, is born ten years before *O* conveys. Five years after *O* conveys, *A* appoints to *B* for life, then to such of *B*'s children as *B* shall appoint. When *B*'s first child, *C*, is born 25 years after *O*'s conveyance, *B* appoints to *C* and his heirs.

386.   At the time of the conveyance, what is *A*'s power of appointment?
387.   At the time of *A*'s appointment, what is *B*'s power of appointment?
388.   What is *C*'s interest now?

O conveys to *A* for life, then to such of *A*'s issue as *A* shall appoint, and in default of appointment to *S*. *A*'s child, *B*, is born ten years after *O* conveys. Thirty-five years after *O* conveys, *A* appoints to *B* for life, then to such of *B*'s children as *B* shall appoint. *B* immediately appoints to *C*, his first child.

389.   At the time of the conveyance, what is *A*'s power of appointment?
390.   At the time of *A*'s appointment, what is *B*'s power of appointment?
391.   What is *C*'s interest now?

O devises to his wife, *A*, for life, then to whomever *A* shall appoint. *A* dies ten years later, devising to her children and grandchildren alive at *A*'s death for the life of their survivor, and on the death of the survivor of this group, to that person's children. When *A* dies, she leaves two children, ages 30 and 33, and three grandchildren, ages five, seven, and eleven.

392.   What is the interest of the children of the survivor?

O devises Blackacre to *A* for life, then to such issue of *A* as *A* shall appoint, and in default of appointment to *S*. *A* appoints to his child *B* (born after *O*'s death) for life, remainder to *B*'s children. *B* does not yet have children.

393. What is *B*'s interest?
394. What is the interest of *B*'s children?

O devises Blackacre to *A* for life, then to such issue of *A* as *A* shall appoint, and in default of appointment to *S*. *A* appoints to his child *B* (born after *O*'s death) for life, remainder to *B*'s children who shall be born within 21 years of *A*'s life. *B* does not yet have children.

395. What is the interest of *B*'s children?

O conveys to *A* for life, then to such persons as *A* shall appoint. *A* then has a child, *B*. Upon his death, *A* appoints the property to *B* for life, then to such of *B*'s children as *B* shall appoint. *B* bears a child, *C*, and immediately appoints the property to *C* to take effect upon *B*'s death.

396. At the time of the conveyance, what is *A*'s power of appointment?
397. At the time of *A*'s appointment, what is *B*'s power of appointment?
398. What is *C*'s interest now?

O conveys to *A* for life, then to such persons as *A* shall by will appoint. *A*'s wife bears a child, *B*. Upon his death, *A* appoints the property to *B* for life, then to such of *B*'s children as *B* shall appoint. *B* has a child, *C*, and immediately appoints the property to *C* to take effect upon *B*'s death.

399. At the time of the conveyance, what is *A*'s power of appointment?
400. At the time of *A*'s appointment, what is *B*'s power of appointment?
401. What is *C*'s interest now?

O conveys to *A* for life, then to *A*'s widow for life, then to the then surviving children of *A* for their joint lives, then to such grandchildren of *A* as *A* shall appoint, and in default of appointment to *S*. *A* loses his wife in a plane crash and dies one year later of a heart attack. On his death *A* appoints by will to all the children of his son *B*. *B* was born after *O*'s conveyance and is still alive. *B* has two children, *X* and *Y*.

402. What is *B*'s interest now?
403. At the time of the conveyance, what is *A*'s power of appointment?
404. What is *X*'s interest now?

O conveys Blackacre to *A* for life, then to *A*'s children for their joint lives, then to *A*'s grandchildren as the first child of *A* shall appoint, and in default of appointment to *S*. Two years later *A* has his first child, *B*, and 15 years after that, *A* has his first grandchild, *X*. On *X*'s third birthday, *B* appoints the remainder in Blackacre to *X*.

405. At the time of the conveyance, what is the power of appointment of *A*'s first child?
406. What is *X*'s interest now?

O conveys to *A* for life, then to such persons as *A* shall appoint. *A* immediately appoints to *A*'s children for their joint lives, then to *A*'s grandchildren. Two years later *A* has her first child.

> 407. At the time of the conveyance, what is *A*'s power of appointment?
>
> 408. What is the interest of *A*'s grandchildren now?

O conveys to *A* for life, then to all the children of *A* in such shares as *A* shall appoint, and in default of appointment to *B* and his heirs. *A* appoints by will to *X*, the oldest of his three children.

> 409. At the time of the conveyance, what is *A*'s power of appointment?
>
> 410. What is *X*'s interest now?
>
> 411. What is *B*'s interest now?

O conveys to *A* for life, then to the children of *A* as *A* shall appoint. *A* immediately appoints a life estate to *X*. *A* has three children, *X* (age 25), *Y* (age 23), and *Z* (age 21).

> 412. At the time of the conveyance, what is *A*'s power of appointment?
>
> 413. What is the interest of the children of *A* now?
>
> 414. What is *X*'s estate now?

O conveys to *A* for life, then to the children of *B* for the life of the survivor, then to such children of *C* as *A* shall by deed appoint. At the time of the conveyance, neither *B* nor *C* have had children. Over the next ten years *C* has three children, *X*, *Y*, and *Z*. *C* exercises her power of appointment by leaving in her will upon her death the whole of the appointive property to *X* for life.

> 415. At the time of the conveyance, what is *A*'s power of appointment?
>
> 416. At the time of the conveyance, what is the interest of *C*'s children?
>
> 417. What is *X*'s estate now?

O conveys to *A* for life, then to such children of *A* as *A* by will may direct. Upon *A*'s death, *A* has two sons, *X* and *Y*. *A*'s will contains a residuary clause giving all property she owns or has control over to *X*. There is no specific mention of the power of appointment nor of *O*'s property, although *A* knew she had the power of appointment, executed her will with the orally expressed purpose to exercise the power, and died without owning any other property.

> 418. At the time of the conveyance, what is *A*'s power of appointment?
>
> 419. What is *X*'s unshared interest now?

O conveys to *A* for life, then to such persons as *A* shall by will appoint. Upon her death ten years later, *A* appoints to *A*'s children for the life of the survivor, then to the grandchildren of *A*. At the time of *A*'s death, *A*'s children are *X* (age 30) and *Y* (age eleven); *X* has one child, *G* (age three).

420.   At the time of the conveyance, what is *A*'s power of appointment?

421.   What is the interest of the unborn grandchildren now?

O conveys to *A* for life, then to *A*'s widow for life, then to such persons as *A*'s widow should appoint. *A* has a wife.

422.   What is the power of appointment of *A*'s widow?

O conveys to *A* and the heirs of her body, then to such children of *B* as *A*'s first child should appoint by deed, and in default of appointment to *C* if *C* is married. Neither *A* nor *B* have ever had children.

423.   What is the power of appointment of *A*'s first child?
424.   What is *C*'s interest?

O devises to his wife, *A*, for life, then, one year later, to whomever *A* shall by will appoint, and in default of appointment, to *A*'s grandchildren when they reach 30 years of age. *A* fails to appoint and at her death (six years after *O*'s conveyance) her children are all dead, although she does have a one and only grandchild, age three.

425.   What is the interest of the grandchild?

Answers

376.   *L. Fee simple absolute.* The unrestricted power in the conveyance is consistent with a fee simple absolute. There is really no power created in this conveyance other than the power inherent in a fee simple absolute.

377.   *C. Life estate. A*'s general testamentary power of appointment in the conveyance, coupled with the gift over in default of appointment, does not extend *A*'s life estate into a fee simple absolute. The gift over in default of appointment is a vested remainder in *X* in fee simple subject to executory limitation.

378.   *F. Vested remainder* in fee simple subject to executory limitation. The power of appointment makes the vested remainder subject to complete divestment. *A* has a special testamentary power of appointment that is exclusive because he is not required to appoint to all his children.

379.   *F. Valid special power of appointment exercisable by deed or will.* It is valid under the RAP because it may be exercised only before *X*, *Y*, and *Z* (lives in being at the creation of the power) die.

380.   *F. Vested remainder* in a life estate pur autre vie. At the time of the conveyance, *A* has a life estate, *A*'s oldest child (before birth) has a contingent remainder for life, and *S* has a vested remainder in fee simple subject to executory limitation. When *B* is born, *B* takes a vested remainder in a life estate. When *B* exercises her power of appointment, the appointment cuts short *S*'s estate

and creates a vested remainder in *X*. This appointed interest is valid under the RAP because it is a remainder that vests in *X* (a life in being at the creation of the power).

381. I. *Invalid general power of appointment exercisable by deed or will.* The power is invalid under the RAP because it may be acquired beyond the perpetuities period. *A* may have a child, *P*, after *O*'s conveyance. Then *A* and all lives in being at the time of the conveyance may die. *P* may not have a child (*A*'s first grandchild) until more than 21 years later, at which time the power would be acquired too late. It does not matter what actually did happen; only what might have happened.

382. I. *None.* At the time of the conveyance, *A* has a life estate, *A*'s grandchildren have a contingent remainder in a life estate pur autre vie (for the life of the first to die), and *O* has a reversion. Since the power is invalid, there can be no appointment. Note that the grandchildren's contingent remainder is safe from the RAP because of the Destructibility of Contingent Remainders Rule.

383. C. *Valid general power of appointment exercisable by deed or will.* It is valid under the RAP because *A*'s oldest child can acquire it only upon birth to *A*, a life in being at the creation of the power.

384. B. *Executory interest* in fee simple absolute. At the time of the conveyance, *A* has a life estate, *A*'s oldest child has a contingent remainder for life, and *O* has a reversion in fee simple subject to executory limitation. When *A*'s oldest child, *X*, is born, *X* takes a vested remainder. When *X* exercises her power of appointment, the appointment is still contingent on the birth of a child to *B*; therefore, it does not cut short *O*'s estate but creates an executory interest that stands ready to cut short *O*'s estate. This appointed interest is valid because *B* is a life in being at the time of the appointment and the interest of *B*'s children becomes vested upon birth to *B*.

385. B. *Executory interest* in fee simple absolute. At the time of the devise, *A* has a life estate, *O*'s heirs have *O*'s reversion in fee simple subject to executory limitation, and *A*'s grandchildren have an executory interest in fee simple subject to executory limitation. At the time of the devise, *A* also has a general power of appointment exercisable by deed or will that is valid under the RAP because it is acquired immediately. The power, if exercised, would have cut short the estate in *A*'s grandchildren one year after *A*'s death. When *A* dies without having exercised her power, *O*'s heirs have a present interest in fee simple subject to executory limitation, and *A*'s grandchildren have an executory interest in fee simple absolute. In default of appointment, *A*'s grandchildren are designated to take one year after *A*'s life estate when they reach 30. Their interest is valid under the RAP because the RAP is applied at the time that the power expires on *A*'s death. At that time the one and only grandchild is a life in being, and her interest will vest, if at all, within her lifetime.

386. *F. Valid special power of appointment exercisable by deed or will*, which is exclusive. It is valid under the RAP because it may be exercised only in *A*'s lifetime or upon *A*'s death, and *A* is a life in being at the creation of the power.

387. *F. Valid special power of appointment exercisable by deed or will*, which is exclusive. It is valid under the RAP because it may be exercised only in *B*'s lifetime or upon *B*'s death, and *B* is a life in being at the creation of the power (considered to be the time of conveyance under the relation back doctrine).

388. *F. Vested remainder* in fee simple absolute. At the time of *O*'s conveyance, *A* has a life estate and *S* has a vested remainder in fee simple subject to executory limitation. *A* also has a power that is exercised in favor of *B*, a life in being at the time of *O*'s conveyance, to give *B* a vested remainder in a life estate and a power of appointment. The exercise of *B*'s power in favor of *C* gives *C* a vested remainder to follow *B*'s life estate. Reading this interest back into *O*'s conveyance, it is designated to take upon the death of *A* or *B*, who are lives in being at the time of *O*'s conveyance. Therefore, it is valid under the RAP.

389. *F. Valid special power of appointment exercisable by deed or will*, which is exclusive. It is valid under the RAP because it may be exercised only in *A*'s lifetime or upon *A*'s death, and *A* is a life in being at the creation of the power.

390. *L. Invalid special power of appointment exercisable by deed or will*. *A*'s power is exercised in favor of *B*, a life *not* in being at the time of *O*'s conveyance, to give *B* a vested remainder in a life estate. This interest created by *A*'s power of appointment is valid because it is a remainder that, when read into the conveyance at the time *A*'s power was created, must vest on or before the death of *A*, a life in being at that time. *A*'s power is also exercised in favor of *B* in an attempt to give *B* a power of appointment. *B*'s power is invalid under the RAP because, when read into the conveyance at the time *A*'s power was created (that is, the time of conveyance), it is possible for this power to be exercised beyond the perpetuities period. One may hypothesize that *B*, who is not a life in being at the time of the conveyance, may exercise this power more than 21 years after the death of every life in being to give a remainder following his own interest.

391. *I. None*. At the time of the conveyance, *A* has a life estate and *S* has a vested remainder in fee simple subject to executory limitation. At the time of *A*'s appointment, *A* has a life estate, *B* has a vested remainder in a life estate, and *S* has a vested remainder in fee simple absolute. At the time of *B*'s appointment, the interests remain the same. *B*'s appointment is invalid because his power is invalid. See problem 390 above.

392. *B. Executory interest* in fee simple absolute. At the time of the devise, *A* has a life estate and a general power of appointment exercisable by deed or will. *O*'s heirs have *O*'s reversion in fee simple subject to executory limitation. *A*'s power is valid because it is acquired at the time it is created. *A*'s power is

exercised by will to give her surviving children and grandchildren a present interest in a life estate pur autre vie (for the life of the survivor) and to give the children of the survivor a contingent interest (contingent on identification of the survivor and birth of the children) in fee simple absolute. The contingent interest is an executory interest rather than a contingent remainder because it is an appointed interest that must cut short *O*'s heirs' estate in order to vest. (This analysis is dictated by consistency with problem 395 below.) Both the present interest and the executory interest are valid because the RAP is applied from the time the appointed interests are created. The survivor is a life in being at that time and the survivor's children take, if at all, a vested interest no later than the death of the survivor.

393.   *F.   Vested remainder* in a life estate. *A* has a life estate and a special exclusive power of appointment exercisable by deed or will. The power is valid because it must be exercised no later than *A*'s death. The exercise of the appointment giving *B* a vested remainder is valid under the RAP because, viewed from the time of the devise but using the second look doctrine, it will vest at the time of *A*'s appointment which occurs during the life of *A*, a life in being at the time of *O*'s devise.

394.   *I.   None. A* attempted to give *B*'s children a contingent interest but this interest is invalid under the RAP. One may hypothesize that all lives in being at the time of *O*'s death may die and *B* may have children more than 21 years later, thus vesting their interest too late. Therefore, following *B*'s vested remainder in a life estate, *S* holds a vested remainder in fee simple absolute.

395.   *B.   Executory interest* in fee simple absolute. The analysis is the same as in problems 393 and 394 above, except that *B*'s children get a valid interest because their interest must vest, if at all, within 21 years of a life in being at the time of *O*'s devise. Therefore, *A* has a present interest in a life estate, *B* has a vested remainder in a life estate, *S* has a vested remainder in fee simple subject to executory limitation, and *B*'s children have an executory interest that stands ready to cut short *S*'s estate upon the birth of a child to *B* within 21 years of the death of *A*. Note that *B*'s children cannot have a contingent remainder because such a contingent remainder would divest *S*'s vested remainder if the contingency is satisfied, and such a divestment is not permitted under the Backup Rule.

396.   *C.   Valid general power of appointment exercisable by deed or will. A* has a life estate and a power of appointment. The power is valid under the RAP because it is acquired at the same time that the power is created.

397.   *F.   Valid special power of appointment exercisable by deed or will*, which is exclusive. *A*'s appointment gives *B* a present interest in a life estate and a power of appointment. The validity of this appointed interest and this appointed power is determined by applying the RAP from the time of *A*'s death when the ap-

pointment is made. The present interest in *B* is valid because it vests at the time of *A*'s death. *B*'s power is valid because it must be exercised, if at all, by *B*, a life in being at the time of *A*'s death.

398.   *F.   Vested remainder* in fee simple absolute. *B*'s appointment gives *C* a valid interest under the RAP because, reading *C*'s interest back into *A*'s will but using the second look doctrine, *C* has a remainder that vests at the time of *B*'s appointment while *B*, a life in being at *A*'s death, is alive.

399.   *A.   Valid general testamentary power of appointment. A* has a life estate and a power of appointment. The power is valid under the RAP because it must be exercised, if at all, no later than the death of a *A*, a life in being at the time of *O*'s conveyance.

400.   *L.   Invalid special power of appointment exercisable by deed or will. A*'s appointment gives *B* a present interest in a life estate and attempts to give *B* a power of appointment. *B*'s present interest is valid because it vests upon the death of *A*, a life in being at the time of *O*'s conveyance. The validity of the appointed power is also determined by applying the RAP from the time of *O*'s conveyance when *A*'s power was created. The special power is given to *B*, who is not a life in being at the time of *O*'s conveyance. This power may be exercised beyond the perpetuities period as measured from that time. Therefore, *B*'s power is invalid under the RAP.

401.   *I.   None.* Since *B*'s power is invalid, the appointed interest under *B*'s power is invalid. There is presently a life estate in *B* and a reversion in *O*.

402.   *I.   None.* At the time of *O*'s conveyance *A* has a present interest in a life estate, *A*'s widow has a contingent remainder for life, and *S* has a vested remainder in fee simple subject to executory limitation. The attempted conveyance of a contingent remainder to the children of *A* is invalid because *A*'s widow and *A*'s surviving children may not be lives in being at the time of *O*'s conveyance and the widow may hold a present life estate for more than 21 years after which it may vest in the surviving children too late.

403.   *F.   Valid special power of appointment exercisable by deed or will,* which is exclusive. The power is valid because it must be exercised no later than the death of *A*, a life in being at the time of *O*'s conveyance.

404.   *F.   Vested remainder* in a fee simple absolute. The exercise of *A*'s power is valid because, taking into consideration the facts existing at the time the appointment is made, the grandchildren, *X* and *Y*, take a present interest immediately upon the death of *A*, a life in being at the time of *O*'s conveyance, and the class is closed to future grandchildren.

405.   *L.   Invalid special power of appointment exercisable by deed or will. O* attempts to give *B*, unborn at the time of the conveyance, a power of appointment. The power is invalid under the RAP because, it may be exercised beyond the perpetuities period.

One may hypothesize that all lives in being at the time of the conveyance may die, and *B* may exercise the power more than 21 years later to give grandchildren an interest.

406.   I.   *None. A* has a life estate, *A*'s children have a contingent remainder in a life estate pur autre vie (for the life of the first to die), and *S* has a vested remainder in fee simple absolute.

407.   C.   *Valid general power of appointment exercisable by deed or will.* *A* has a life estate and a power of appointment. The power is valid under the RAP because it is acquired at the same time that the power is created.

408.   I.   *None. A*'s power is exercised to give a contingent interest in a life estate pur autre vie (for the life of the first to die) to *A*'s children. This interest is valid because the children will take a vested interest upon birth to *A*, a life in being at the time *A* exercises her appointment. The attempt to give an interest to *A*'s grandchildren fails under the RAP because they may take their interest beyond the perpetuities period as measured from the time of *A*'s appointment. One may hypothesize that the children who are not lives in being at the time of *A*'s appointment may live more than 21 years beyond the deaths of all lives in being at that time, then a grandchild would be born whose interest would vest too late. Therefore, the interest of the grandchildren is void. At the time of *A*'s appointment, *A* has a life estate, *O* has a reversion in fee simple subject to executory limitation, and *A*'s children (yet unborn) have an executory interest in a life estate pur autre vie. After *A* has her first child, *A* has a life estate, *A*'s first child has a vested remainder subject to open in a life estate pur autre vie, and *O* has a reversion in fee simple absolute.

409.   F.   *Valid special power of appointment exercisable by deed or will.* It is nonexclusive because *A*'s appointment must include all the children. It is valid because it must be exercised by *A* who is a life in being at the time of the conveyance.

410.   I.   *None.* At the time of the conveyance *A* has a life estate and *B* has a vested remainder subject to complete divestment, more specifically stated as a vested remainder in fee simple subject to executory limitation. The exercise of *A*'s power excludes two of *A*'s children and thus renders the appointment completely invalid.

411.   A.   *Present interest* in a fee simple absolute. The failure of *A*'s appointment upon *A*'s death triggers the gift over in default. Therefore, *B*'s estate is no longer subject to executory limitation.

412.   F.   *Valid special power of appointment exercisable by deed or will,* which is exclusive.

413.   H.   *Vested remainder subject to open* in fee simple absolute. At the time of the conveyance, *A* has a life estate, and *A*'s children who are born have a vested remainder subject to open because they are implied takers in default of appointment. After the partial

414. appointment, they continue to be implied takers in default of appointment with a remainder following *X*'s remainder.

414. *Q.* *None of the above is correct.* *A*'s exercise of the power of appointment is valid under the RAP because it creates an interest that is immediately vested in *X* at a time when *A*, a life in being at the creation of the power, is alive. It is only a partial exercise of *A*'s power, but this is permitted. *X* takes a vested remainder in a life estate following *A*'s life estate. But *X* also shares in the fee simple absolute shared by all the children as implied takers in default of appointment. See problem 413 above.

415. *E.* *Valid special power of appointment exercisable by deed,* which is exclusive. It is valid under the RAP because it cannot be exercised beyond the life of *A*, a life in being at the time the power is created.

416. *D.* *Contingent remainder.* At the time of the conveyance, *A* has a life estate, *B*'s children have a contingent remainder in a life estate pur autre vie, *C*'s children have a contingent remainder (contingent on birth) in a fee simple subject to executory limitation (as implied takers in default of appointment), and *O* has a reversion in fee simple subject to executory limitation.

417. *L.* *Fee simple absolute.* The birth of a child to *C* transforms the contingent remainder in *C*'s children into a vested remainder subject to open in a fee simple subject to executory limitation in the child and into an executory interest in fee simple subject to executory limitation in the unborn children. *O*'s reversion is divested. When *C* attempts to exercise her power of appointment in her will rather than by deed, the appointment is invalid. Therefore, *A* has a life estate, *B*'s children (yet unborn) have a contingent remainder in a life estate pur autre vie, and *C*'s children (*X*, *Y*, and *Z*) share a vested remainder in fee simple absolute as takers in default of appointment. The interest of *C*'s children is no longer subject to open because the class of *C*'s children closes naturally with *C*'s death, and the estate of *C*'s children is no longer subject to executory limitation because the appointment is invalid.

418. *D.* *Valid special testamentary power of appointment,* which is exclusive. The power must be exercised, if at all, at the death of *A*, a life in being at the time the power is created.

419. *A.* *Present interest* in fee simple absolute. Although there generally must be reference in a will to the subject of the power or to the power itself in order to exercise it, an exception is made where the will would be inoperative without the aid of the power and the intention to execute the power was clear and manifest. The exception is applicable in this case. Furthermore, there is no violation of the RAP because *X* takes a vested interest upon the death of *A*, a life in being at the time the power was created. Therefore, the exercise of the power is valid.

420. *A.* *Valid general testamentary power of appointment.* *A* has a life estate and a power of appointment. The power is valid under

the RAP because it must be exercised, if at all, no later than the death of *A*, a life in being at the time of *O*'s conveyance.

421. *B.*   *Executory interest* in fee simple absolute. *A*'s appointment is valid under the RAP because the interests of both the children and the grandchildren must vest, if at all, on or before the death of a life in being at the time of *O*'s conveyance. The "second look" doctrine establishes the fact that all *A*'s children by the time the class closes upon *A*'s death are lives in being at the time of *O*'s conveyance. Their interest vests in their own lifetimes, and the interest of all the grandchildren vests no later than the death of the surviving child. *X* and *Y* have a present interest in a life estate pur autre vie, *G* has a vested remainder subject to open in a fee simple subject to executory limitation, and the unborn grandchildren have an executory interest.

422. *G.*   *Invalid general testamentary power of appointment.* *A* has a life estate, *A*'s widow has a contingent remainder in a life estate, and *O* has a reversion in fee simple absolute. The interest of *A*'s widow is contingent because a widow cannot be determined until *A*'s death. In fact *A*'s widow may not yet be born at the time of *O*'s conveyance. If one hypothesizes that such a widow takes a present interest upon *A*'s death and waits 25 years after the deaths of all lives in being at the time of *O*'s conveyance before exercising her power of appointment, then the exercise would occur too late under the RAP and the power is invalid.

423. *K.*   *Invalid special power of appointment exercisable by deed.* The power is invalid under the RAP because it may be exercised more than 21 years after the death of all lives in being at the time of the conveyance. One may hypothesize that *A*'s first child may be born, all lives in being at the time of the conveyance may die, and *A*'s first child may exercise her appointment more than 21 years later.

424. *D.*   *Contingent remainder* in fee simple absolute. Ordinarily the gift in default of appointment is vested, but *C*'s interest has the condition precedent of marriage. Therefore, *A* has a fee tail, *C* has a contingent remainder, and *O* has a reversion in fee simple absolute.

425. *I.*   *None.* At the time of the devise, *A* has a life estate and *O*'s heirs have *O*'s reversion. At the time of the devise, *A* also has a general testamentary power of appointment that is valid under the RAP because it must be exercised, if at all, no later than the death of *A*, a life in being at the time the power was created. The power, if exercised, would have cut short the estate in *O*'s heirs one year after *A*'s death. In default of appointment, *O* attempted to devise an executory interest to *A*'s grandchildren. In default of appointment, they were designated to take one year after *A*'s life estate when they reached 30, but their interest is void under the RAP. Even giving a "second

look" at the facts that existed at the time of *A*'s death, one may hypothesize that after *A*'s death all lives in being at the time of *O*'s devise die, and more than 21 years pass before *A*'s grandchild takes a vested interest. Therefore, at *A*'s death *O*'s heirs take a present interest in fee simple absolute because the power has not been exercised and the gift over in default of appointment is void.